AA Truck
Suppleme
To
Restorer's
MODEL A
SHOP MANUAL
Jim Schild

D0732023

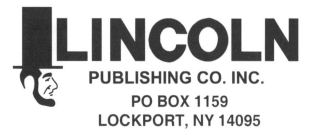

LINCOLN
PUBLISHING CO. INC.
PO BOX 1159
LOCKPORT, NY 14095

Library of Congress Cataloging in Publication Data

Schild, Jim
AA Supplement to Restorer's Model A Shop Manual

Bibliography: p.
1. Automobiles - Conservation & Restoration
2. Ford Automobiles. I. Title

629.28   93-71706
ISBN: 0-9624958-5-9

The Auto Review P.O. Box 510, Florissant, MO 63032

97 96 95   9 8 7 6 5 4 3

PREFACE

The concept for this supplement came soon after the completion of the original **Restorer's Model A Shop Manual** in 1985. It has taken a long time to put this supplement together because of other commitments such as my Classic Car Shop Manual and active duty for Desert Storm. Each year, I planned to finish this book, and each year something else would get in the way. As I continued to get requests for this book from Model A truck fans, and as interest in AA trucks grew, I kept pushing myself to gather everything needed to complete the project.

I must make it clear from the start that this book is not meant to be used alone, but only as a supplement to the Model A Shop Manual. The chapters and information are identified as they relate to the chapters and information in the original shop manual. I have tried not to include anything in here that is already included in the other book.

In addition to the information directly related to the AA, I have also included a detailed chapter on body work and finishing that was not included in the original shop manual due to publisher requirements. This up-to-date information was taken in part from the extensive body chapter in my Classic Car Shop Manual and adapted to the AA Body.

As with the original Model A Shop Manual, this book should be used in conjunction with the latest MARC/MAFCA Judging standards and the appropriate Ford Parts Price List and Service Bulletins which are available from Classic Motorbooks and from most Model A parts dealers.

Like the Model A Manual, this book is not intended to have all of the answers, but every owner and restorer of AA trucks will find something that will help make their task a little easier and hopefully, owning their Ford a little more fun.

Jim Schild

CONTENTS

SUPPLEMENT TO
Chapter 3

WHEELS HUBS AND BRAKES

AA truck wheels took on at least six different forms. The first was the AA-1015-AR spoke wheel; the second was the AA-1015-BR Ford six hole disc wheel; the third was the AA-1015-C (later BB-1015-A) Budd disc wheel. This wheel took three forms with changes being made in January and April of 1931. These changes are explained on pages 527 and 552 of the 1931 Ford Service Bulletins. The final standard design, used only on certain 1931 models, was the AA-1015-E 20 inch spoke wheel. There was also a seldom seen AA-1015-F (later BB-1015-B) eighteen inch wheel used for the optional 32 x 7 tire. The date of manufacture of all Budd wheels may be found stamped on the inside mounting surface near the lug bolt holes. This date will sometimes help date a truck.

All AA truck wheels were of the semi-split rim snap ring type. The 20 inch five hole disc wheels were made by the Budd Wheel Corporation and were similar in design to those used by many other truck makers at the time. The various wheel types also needed a variety of lug nuts to secure them to the hubs. The first type was the AA-1120-AR/AA1121-AR used on the early 1928 spoke wheels. Although the factory parts book only lists one part number for these fasteners, there were actually two different types used. One had a design similar to the AR car lug nuts while the other was an acorn type. When the Budd-type offset disc wheels were introduced in late 1929, the AA-1120/21-B (later BB-1120/21) nut was introduced along with it. This assembly incorporated the AA-1132/33 (later BB-1132/33) inner nut and special outer nut AA-1143/35 (later BB-1134/35) to secure the rear duals available with the Budd wheels. All AA trucks had left hand threads on the left side and right hand threads on the right side.

AA-1015-AR Ford 20 inch spoke wheel used on early trucks.

The wheel is attached by five exposed AA-1120-AR/AA-1121-AR lug nuts.

AA-1015-BR Ford 20 inch disc wheel. Notice the six vent holes.

Outside manufacturers made many varieties of wheel for the Ford truck. These are demountable rim type on a 1929 AA.

This is the first type AA-1015-C 20 inch Budd wheel. Notice the five vent holes.

AA-1015-C wheel in the latest 1931 variation. Notice the reinforcing rim around the center.

This 20 inch snap ring is used on all 20 inch AA wheels. It should be installed by an experienced professional shop.

An example of the 20 inch AA-1015-E spoke wheel used on the 1931 AA-Ambulance and Funeral coach. It is compared here with a 19 inch Model A wheel.

This is the AA-1015-E wheel with the snap ring installed

Notice that the AA-1015-E wheel has much heavier spokes than the car wheel.

Restoration of the wheels

As with any restoration the first step any restoration operation is to clean and inspect the wheels for excessive rust or defects. The most common defects in Ford truck wheels are cracks near the hub bolt holes and rust out of the rims found especially around the valve stem holes. Ford truck wheels can be cleaned very well by either sandblasting or acid dipping. They are very strong and usually are not susceptible to weakening as are car parts.

Dipping is usually the best choice for spoke wheels since sandblasting cannot always reach every surface and the acid dip solution will not leave a rough surface as will the sandblasting. If any of the rims are rusted out at the valve stem openings and better wheels cannot be found, they should have the holes welded closed entirely and new ones drilled at another place on the rim. Notice that these holes are usually elongated rather than round so that the bent metal stem will enter easily.

Inspect the wheels to insure that they are round and do not have any excessive rim dents or flat spots. Both the spoke and the disc wheels were originally finished to a smooth high gloss. The outer disc surface of the Budd and Ford wheels are usually badly pitted as found today and this surface will have to be repaired. It can be remedied with a few brushed on coatings of R.S.P. Quik-Poly available from T-Distributing in St. Charles, Missouri. After sanding, the wheels may then be primed with PPG DP-40 Epoxy primer and K200/K201 primer-surfacer and sanded until the desired finish is attained. The wheels should then be painted with a good quality hardened enamel or PPG Deltron acrylic urethane for durability and chip resistance. See the paint manufacturer's directions for proper application and safety precautions of these finishes. Most truck wheels should be painted black, but in 1931, fleet orders may have had wheels painted in any color the customer desired.

Tires

When the 1929 Ford AA truck was introduced, the standard tire was a 30 x 5 in front and a 32 x 6 in the rear. These were heavy duty truck tires in all

instances. The 30 x 5 is equivalent to a 500-20 balloon size and the 32 x 6 is equal to a 650-20. In October, 1929, 600-20 6 ply balloon tires became standard equipment along with the introduction of the positive offset Budd disc wheels. In January, 1930, the dual rear wheel option became available for all applications. By 1931, additional tire options included 650-20 front and rear, 600-20 balloon rear duals, 32 x 6 high pressure duals and the 32 x 7 10 ply high pressure singles on 18 inch wheels for the rear.

Mounting tires on the rims

Ford AA truck wheels are all of the semi-split rim snap ring type and should be mounted only by trained and experienced personnel with the proper equipment. Wheel snap rings can be very dangerous if not handled properly. If the tires are not inflated inside a safety cage, the rim can come loose and become a deadly missile. A test by the Tire Safety Commission showed that a tire inflated to only 60 pounds could throw a sixteen pound bowling ball over sixty feet with a force that could decapitate a person easily. Please do not try to mount the tires yourself. Most truck tire dealers will mount these tires for a small charge. Be sure that the proper tubes and flaps are in place when new tires are mounted. The flaps are to prevent the possibly sharp surfaces of the inner rim from puncturing the tube.

When buying tubes, be sure that the proper metal valve stems are installed. A rubber stem will not clear the brake drums unless it is the newer bendable type. Always check to see that the tube is a center stem type. Some tubes are made for automobile applications and have offset stem mountings that will not work on a truck wheel. Metal stems, of course are the only authentic type to use on any pre-1933 vehicle. The original stems on the AA were the TR32 and TR34 double bend configuration in order to fit and function in disc wheel assemblies. These correct stems may not be readily available, but even the more common bent metal stems will work better than rubber stems. See the latest revisions of the MARC/MAFCA Judging Standards for the correct illustrations of the AA stems.

The brake system

The early 1928 brake system had 14 inch AA-1114-AR truck drums in the rear on the vehicles without separate brakes. The front drums were the same diameter as the car brakes, but were AA-1102-AR type to mount the truck wheels. When the separate parking brake system was introduced in early 1928, the rear drums were changed to the AA-1114-BR type.

In October, 1929, when the new heavy duty front axle was introduced, the front brakes were changed to the AA-1102-C and AA-1103-C type which changed the front drums to the same 14 inch diameter as the rear brakes. This was the same time that the wheels were changed to the Budd 5 hole offset disc type.

The truck brake system is very similar in design and operation to the car brake system. The early 131 1/2 inch wheelbase chassis had an extra brake shaft rod and AA-2521 rear rocker arm assembly. When the heavy duty chassis was introduced in the last part of 1929, one of the improvements was

a sturdier brake pedal used only on the AA chassis and listed as AA-2455.

Although many of the truck brake parts are the same as the car, some of the more obvious differences are the brake pedal to cross-shaft rods AA-2465-AR (15-13/16 in.) for the 1928-29 models and the AA-2465-B (25-1/8 in.) for the 1930-31 models. The 157 inch wheelbase chassis used the AA-2465-C (50-5/8 in.) rod. The rear brake rods for both service and parking brakes were different for the truck and these variations may be found in the Ford parts price list. The front rods on most models are the same as the car. What this means to the restorer is that new brake rods are not available for the rear and the old ones will have to be restored or car brake rods modified for use on the AA truck. Remember the safety importance of the brake system when doing any welding or modifying of brake rods. The text will describe other areas where differences exist between the car and the truck parts.

1928 AA-1114-AR rear(left) and AA-1102-AR front brake drums and hubs.

(Left and above) A comparison of the early pressed steel(left) and later cast iron(right) versions of the AA-1102/1103-C front drums. Notice the difference in the rim and the small square weight on the outer rim of the cast iron drum. This drum was taken from a very late chassis number truck built in March, 1932.

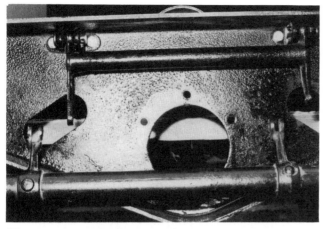

The emergency brake cross shaft AA-2828-C(top) and the service brake cross shaft AA-2485-F attached to the center crossmember

The service brake cross shaft is attached to the frame by AA-2478-B brackets which mount similar to the corresponding car brackets.

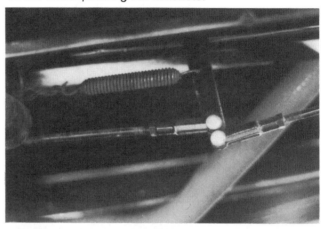

A wider view of the 157 inch frame crossmember with brake cross shafts attached.

AA-2521-B rear brake rocker arm on a 1928 chassis. Notice the AA-2523-R rocker arm retracting spring.

The service brake rod AA-2465-C and emergency brake rod AA-2853-H installed to the cross shafts.

10

The 25 7/16 inch AA-2511 cross shaft to brake rocker arm rod attached to the AA-2521-B front brake rocker arm on a 157 inch chassis. Notice the tailpipe bracket attached to the frame rail.

Rebuilding of the brake system

The rebuilding of the truck brake system follows exactly the same procedures as the car brakes as outlined in RESTORER'S MODEL A SHOP MANUAL. The front brakes assemblies are removed and installed in the same manner as the car brakes except that the left side lug nuts and axle nuts are left-handed threads. The rear brakes are somewhat different than the car due to the different method of removing the rear drums.

Removal of the rear brake assemblies

1. Disconnect the service and emergency brake rods at the levers by removing the cotter pins and clevis pins. Remove the screw off hub cap from the rear hub and remove the cotter pin and 1 3/8 in. hex head nut. Using a suitable large wheel puller, remove the rear hubs from the axle. In some cases, the brakes may be backed off sufficiently to allow the brake drums to be removed by hand without the aid of a puller. Remove the axle key.

2. Remove the cotter pin holding the emergency brake toggle link to the toggle lever. Remove the two springs securing the emergency brake band assembly and remove the emergency brake band.

3. Remove the cotter pin and clevis pin behind the backing plate and remove the toggle lever and shaft from the outside of the brake carrier.

4. Remove the cotter pins and six 11/16 in. castle nuts and remove the BB-2600 carrier assembly from the backing plate.

5. Remove the brake retracting springs using a suitable brake tool and slide the brake shoe link out of the adjusting wedge housing to remove the brake shoes. The backing plate may also now be removed from the axle housing. Be careful not to lose the small spring inside of the service brake operating lever shaft

6. Remove the cotter pins and clevis pins to disassemble the brake shoes for relining.

7. Carefully drive out the rivets and remove the lining material from the brake shoes. It is a simple matter to take these brake shoes to a good brake shop and have new lining fitted and installed in the same manner as indicated in the car shop manual. Of course, the drums should be taken with the brake shoes to be turned and the shoes fitted to the new drum surface.

8. Screw the brake adjusting wedges all the way into the housing and tap on the end to drive out the adjusting wedge housing cap. The adjusting wedge may now be removed and cleaned or replaced as necessary.

Removing the AA-2636 emergency brake toggle lever from the carrier plate after the toggle lever connection has been removed.

AA-2211-B rear brake housing assembly.

AA-2600 emergency brake carrier plate

Notice the small AA-2233 rear brake cam shaft spring when removing the housing.

The carrier plate has been removed to provide access to the service brake shoes and mechanism

The end of the rear axle housing after the brake housing plate has been removed.

Installation of the rear brake assemblies

The installation is the exact reverse of the disassembly. Be sure to use sufficient white lithium brake grease on the adjusting wedges, the brake link and the clevis pins and rollers.

Removal of the front brake assembly

1. Unscrew and remove the hub cap and put it in a safe place.

2. Remove the large cotter pin in the axle nut and remove the 1 1/2 in. axle nut and washer.

3. Remove the front brake drum and hub assembly by pulling it carefully from the spindle. Be careful not to drop the outer wheel bearing. It may be necessary to back off the front brake adjustment to release the drums.

4. Pry the lower ends of the front brake shoes loose and disconnect the springs. Slide the brake adjusting shaft from the adjusting wedge housing and remove the brake shoe assemblies from the backing plate. If the shaft is difficult to remove, tap it out with a hammer.

5. Disconnect the clevis pins and rods from the brake lever. Remove the nut and lockwasher from the front brake shaft housing. Remove the shaft and housing by removing the spindle locking pin and driving the spindle up slightly from the axle. This will loosen the brake shaft housing to where it can be removed without damaging the threads.

(Above) Assembled front brakes on 1931 AA-157 chassis.
(Right) Assembled front brakes on late 1929 AA-131 chassis

6. Remove the nut and cotter pin on the lower rear of the backing plate and remove the brake operating wedge, washer and stud. The brake operating pin will drop out of the spindle as the wedge is removed. Turn the adjusting wedge all the way into the adjusting wedge housing on top of the backing plate and strike the wedge sharply with a hammer to remove it and the housing cover.

7. Remove the four nuts and cotter pins from the back side of the backing plate and remove the backing plate from the spindle.

Inspection and cleaning

Follow the same procedures as outlined on page 30 of the RESTORER'S MODEL A SHOP MANUAL. The reassembly, restoration and adjustment of the front and rear brake assemblies is similar to the procedures described in the car manual. The primary difference is that most of the parts are larger.

AA brake rods

To assist in identifying the numerous brake rods used on the AA truck, the following list gives lengths, part numbers and application where possible.

AA-2465-AR - Brake pedal to cross-shaft rod on early trucks without a separate emergency brake. Length - 15 25/32" to 15 27/32". Diameter - 5/16"

AA-2465-B\C - Brake pedal to cross-shaft rod, 1930-31. Length - 50 9/16" to 50 11/16". Diameter - .310/.314"

AA-2499-AR - Rear brake rod cross-shaft to rear axle. Early 28. Length - 38 1/4". Diameter - .282/.285"

AA-2499-B - Rear brake rod cross-shaft to rear axle. Early 28. length - 37 3/8". Diameter - .282/.285"

AA-2499-CR - Rear brake rod cross-shaft to rear axle. 1928-30. Length - 38". Diameter - .310/.314"

AA-2499-D - Rear brake rod cross-shaft to rear axle. 1930-31. Length - 65 5/16". Diameter - .310/.314"

AA-2500-AR - Rear brake front rod. 1928-29. Length - 39 1/2" to 39 9/16". Diameter - .310/.314"

AA-2500-BR - Rear brake front rod. 1928-29. Length - 35 5/8" to 35 11/16". Diameter - .310/.314"

AA-2501 - Brake rod, cross-shaft to front axle. 1930-31. Length - 61 5/8". Diameter - 5/16"

AA-2511 - Brake rod, cross-shaft to rocker arm, AA157. 1930-31. Length - 25 7/16". Diameter - .310/.314"

AA-2853-AR - Emergency brake lever to cross shaft rod. 1928-29. Length - 29 11/16". Diameter - 5/16"

AA-2853-B - Emergency brake lever to cross-shaft rod. Length - 27 3/16". Diameter - 5/16"

AA-2853-CR - Emergency brake lever to cross-shaft rod. 1929. Length - 27 15/16" to 28 1/16". Diameter - 5/16"

AA-2853-DR - Emergency brake lever to cross-shaft rod. 1929. Length - 28 13/16" to 28 15/16". Diameter - 5/16"

AA-2853-G - Emergency brake lever to cross-shaft rod. 1930. Length - 24 1/4". Diameter - 5/16"

AA-2853-H - Emergency brake lever to cross-shaft rod. AA157 1930. Length - 49 1/4". Diameter - 5/16"

AA-2864-AR - Rod, emergency brake cross-shaft to rear axle. 1928-29. Length - 59 3/4" to 59 7/8". Diameter - 5/16"

AA-2864-B - Rod, emergency brake cross-shaft to rear axle. 1930-31. Length - 63 7/8" to 64". Diameter - 5/16"

All measurements are taken from the centerline of the clevis pin holes.

AA Service Letter Notes

July 24, 1929
Balloon tires have been adopted as standard equipment on the front wheels of the AA trucks. The front tire equipment is now 6.00-20 heavy duty six-ply balloon tires mounted on the standard five inch truck rim.

September 22, 1930
With the first type of rear hub and drum assembly AA-1113-14-D used on the present AA truck, the tread width is 54 inches. Shortly after we started production of this type, the design was changed to increase the tread width to 55-1/2 inches. The AA-1113-14-D rear hub and drum assembly will not be supplied for service so dealers must not allow trucks to operate with one old type and one new type rear hub. If an exchange of only one hub is necessary, replace the other hub and drum assembly at the same time.

January 15, 1931
The AA-1015-C Disc wheel and rim assembly has been changed to provide sufficient side wall clearance for oversize tires when used with dual wheel equipment. The offset has been increased between the centerline of the wheel and the face of the mounting flange from 3-5/8"/3-3/4" to 3-3/4"/3-7/8". Also, the thickness of the bolt flange has been changed from .290/.310" to .315/.335" for increased strength. This change has been in effect since June 1930.

March 10, 1931

The following parts are specified to be used on the Deluxe Police Patrol:

AA-1015-E Wire wheel assembly
AA-1102-E Front hub and drum assembly
AA-1103-E Front hub and drum assembly
AA-1113-G Rear hub and drum assembly
AA-1114-G Rear hub and drum assembly
AA-1137 Wire wheel hub cap
AA-1418 Spare wheel carrier flange assembly
AA-1424 Spare wheel carrier support

The following parts will be reinstated and used in production on the above Model:

AA-1120-A Wheel hub bolt and nut right hand
AA-1121-A Wheel hub bolt and nut left hand
AA-17036-B Starting crank and wheel wrench
A-21924-BS7 Wheel carrier lock nut

April 3, 1931

AA-2011 front brake housing plate and bracket assembly and AA-2211-B rear brake housing plate and bracket assembly have been redesigned in that a slight change has been made in the method of manufacture. In the new design, the brake watershield is integral with the brake housing plate, whereas these parts were separate stampings, riveted and spotwelded together in the old design. The bracket has also been changed slightly to conform to the above change. The new design AA-2022 and AA-2211-B can be used to service the old style brake assemblies or the old style AA-2022 and AA-2211-B can be used with the new style brake assemblies.

July 27, 1931

A new heavy duty high pressure tire, size 32 x 7 will be released as special equipment for those desiring a single wheel and tire capable of carrying the same load as dual 6.00-20 balloons. This tire requires a new wheel 18 x 7 and a special spare wheel mounting which are also furnished as special equipment. The use of this tire increases the tread of the rear wheels 1-1/2" making a tread of 57 inches. Three wheels, two tires and one wheel carrier are to be supplied per set so that the spare wheel will be of the 32 x 7 size. This size can be used to replace the front wheel and tire in emergency cases. It is necessary in all cases to mount the spare wheel and tire on the running board on the driver's side which prevents the use of that door. A new design wheel carrier support is provided for this and the tire rests in a small well which is bolted to the running board. The front fender for this mounting does not require a well. The parts affected by this change are as follows:

AA-1015-F Disc wheel and rim assembly (18") for 32 x 7 tire
AA-1099-B Demountable rim flange (18")
AA-1405-E Spare wheel carrier support
AA-1435 Spare wheel carrier tire well
AA-16514-C Running board assembly RH
AA-16515-C Running board assembly LH

These are the same as AA-16514-B & C except that they have holes for the AA-1435 well. They can be made in your shop.

September 1, 1931

The A-2503 Service brake rod spring has been redesigned in that it has been changed from a flat type spring to a round spring to improve spring action and prevent possibility of breakage. All stock of the flat spring will be used in production and service complaints will be taken care of with the round type spring as soon as the new style springs are available.

Above - 1928-29 AA hub caps. AA-1130-AR(Right) and AA-1130-BR(Left)
Below - 1930-31 AA hub caps. L to R - AA-1131 and AA-1130, cadmium plated.

SUPPLEMENT TO
Chapter 4

FRONT AXLE AND STEERING

THE front axle and steering of the AA truck is similar to that of the passenger car. In fact, the 1928 to early 1929 front axle is the same unit as that used in the Model A car. It should be equipped with a AA-3105-AR spindle to accomodate the truck brake drums and hubs. In late 1929, the new heavy duty axle identified as AA-3010 was introduced. It is considerably larger and heavier than the early unit and no parts will interchange with the earlier unit. Introduction of this axle was accompanied by the introduction of the new, heavier front brakes and brake drum assemblies. See the brake section for identification of these parts.

The new front axle assembly also included a larger AA-3405-B radius rod and heavier spindles BB-3105 and spindle arms. There is not a special truck steering arm or gear as is believed by some. The truck does use a larger BB-3281, Spindle connecting rod (Tie rod).

It is noticeably thicker in the center. Changes in the truck front axle components followed much the same as those of the passenger car.

Inspection of front end and steering

The inspection of the front end and steering is performed exactly as described in the car shop manual pages 41-42.

Removal of the front axle

Removal of the truck front axle is performed exactly as described for the car assemlby except there will be no shock absorber connections on the later truck front end. They were not equipped with front shock absorbers.

16

Disassembly

The disassembly of the front axle is as described for the passenger car except you will notice that on the heavy duty axle, the spindle bearing BB-3123 is mounted below the axle rather than on top as it is on the car.

Inspection and restoration

Inspection and restoration is as described in the car shop manual on pages 44-46. Most good Model A parts dealers now stock the Spindle Bolt kit for the late AA front axle. The reassembly and adjustment of the remainder of the front end is the same as the car except the truck after November, 1929 is designed with a caster setting increased to 3 degrees as shown on page 392 of the Ford Service Bulletins. The toe-in is set to the same amount as the car which is 1/8 inch. See page 47 in the car shop manual for instructions on setting the toe-in.

The steering gear

The AA truck is equipped with the same steering gear as the car and will have all of the accompanying changes as shown in the Judging Standards and the Service Bulletins. The only difference in the trucks is that there may be more of a difference in the date of change because the out-dated parts were generally moved to the truck line. This means you might find a superceded part on a later dated truck that you would not expect to find on a car.

Using a jack and boards to remove the front spring.

Detail of the AA-3131 Spindle arm as installed.

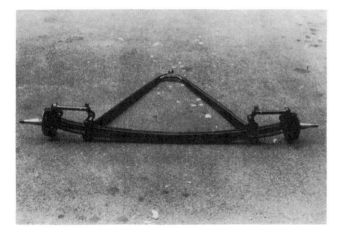

Above and right - Complete 1931 AA front axle assembly

AA Service Letter Notes

April 10, 1929

On all AA trucks built previous to November 1, 1928, such trucks were equipped with the same type front spindles and bearings as used on the Model A car. It has been decided to replace these with the present type heavier AA-3105 spindles and bearings and all dealers should have these changeovers made promptly. To install the heavy type spindle, it is also necessary to change the following parts:

AA-1201 Front wheel inner bearings
AA-1216 Front wheel outer bearings
AA-1102 Hub and drum assembly
AA-1103 Hub and drum assembly
AA-21943 Spindle nut
AA-1120 Hub nuts
AA-1121 Hub nuts
AA-1197 Grease retainer
AA-1195 Grease retainer washer
AA-1190 Dust cap.

The nuts on the rear must also be changed to match so use 10 AA-1120 nuts.

December 9, 1931

A new design steering wheel having more clearance between the belt rail of the body and the rim of the steering wheel is released for use on the Standrive chassis. The rim of the wheel is higher in relation to its hub than the present wheel, making an offset in the throttle control unnecessary. New steering wheels and throttle control rod without offset will be shipped to this branch. Dealers should arrange to change steering wheels and throttle rods on all Standrive chassis assembled in dealer's hands, or in service.

SUPPLEMENT TO
Chapter 5

REAR AXLE

THE rear axle of the AA truck was available in three basic variations. The early 1928 to late 1929 trucks are equipped with a worm drive AA-4000-AR, BR, ER and FR axle assembly of a design similar to that found on the TT trucks. Some of the parts are actually interchangeable with the TT axle. The AA axle part numbers varied according to whether the truck had a 7.25:1 or 5.17:1 gear ratio and whether it was equipped with a separate parking brake.

There was also a seldom seen bevel gear rear axle used on some 1928-29 models with was designed similar to the one used on Model A cars but larger. It had AA-4010-C housings, and gear ratios of 7.16:1 and 5.11:1.

In January, 1930, the truck chassis improvements included an upgraded bevel gear axle assembly. This heavy duty design was a great improvement over the old rear axle and added significantly to the load carrying capacity of the truck. The Ford Service Bulletins describe the axle shafts as being considerably heavier than the old design and said the wheel bearings were increased in length over 33%. This basic axle assembly design was used on Ford trucks at least until 1950.

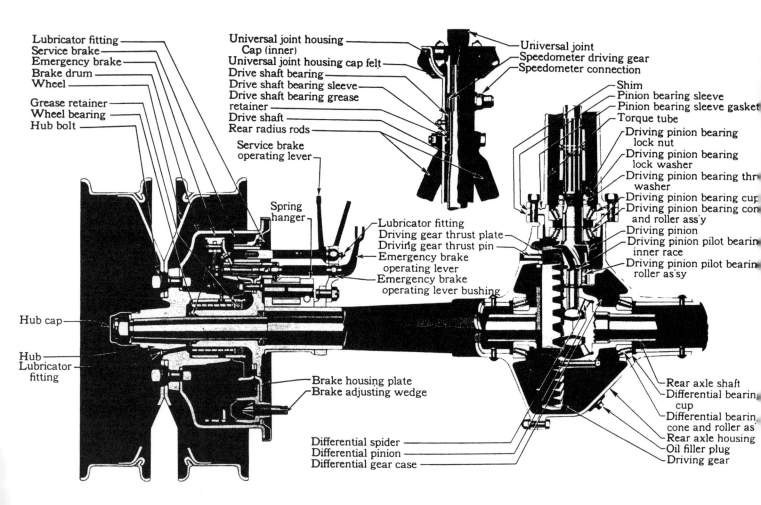

Lubricator fitting
Service brake
Emergency brake
Brake drum
Wheel

Grease retainer
Wheel bearing
Hub bolt

Hub cap

Hub
Lubricator
fitting

Service brake
operating lever

Spring
hanger

Universal joint housing
Cap (inner)
Universal joint housing cap felt
Drive shaft bearing
Drive shaft bearing sleeve
Drive shaft bearing grease
retainer
Drive shaft
Rear radius rods

Universal joint
Speedometer driving gear
Speedometer connection

Shim
Pinion bearing sleeve
Pinion bearing sleeve gasket
Torque tube
Driving pinion bearing
lock nut
Driving pinion bearing
lock washer
Driving pinion bearing thrust
washer
Driving pinion bearing cup
Driving pinion bearing cone
and roller ass'y
Driving pinion
Driving pinion pilot bearing
inner race
Driving pinion pilot bearing
roller as'sy

Lubricator fitting
Driving gear thrust plate
Driving gear thrust pin
Emergency brake
operating lever
Emergency brake
operating lever bushing

Brake housing plate
Brake adjusting wedge

Differential spider
Differential pinion
Differential gear case

Rear axle shaft
Differential bearing
cup
Differential bearing
cone and roller as'
Rear axle housing
Oil filler plug
Driving gear

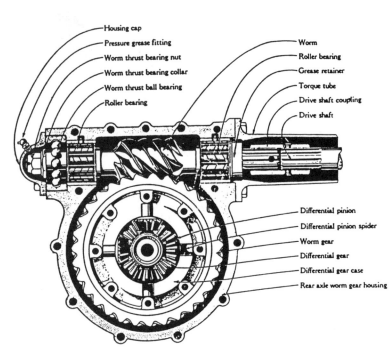

Housing cap
Pressure grease fitting
Worm thrust bearing nut
Worm thrust bearing collar
Worm thrust ball bearing
Roller bearing

Worm
Roller bearing
Grease retainer
Torque tube
Drive shaft coupling
Drive shaft

Differential pinion
Differential pinion spider
Worm gear
Differential gear
Differential gear case
Rear axle worm gear housing

Inspection and troubleshooting

The inspection and troubleshooting of the AA rear axle is the same as in the Model A car.

Removal of the rear axle assembly

1. Drain the lubricant from the rear axle by removing the lower plug on the differential housing. Disconnect the service and emergency brake rods from the brake levers by removing the cotter pins and clevis pins.

2. Disconnect the brake retracting springs from the radius rods by removing the 5/16 inch nuts, bolts and washers from the brackets. If the truck is equipped with the optional AA-18015/AA-18016 shock absorbers, disconnect the shock absorber arms from the shock absorbers by removing the clamp bolt and pulling the arm off of the shaft.

3. Using a 7/8 inch wrench, remove the two 9/16-

18 nuts from the left and right rear spring seat assemblies and remove the lower half of the seat. Using a sturdy jack, raise the frame of the truck high enough for the spring seat upper half to clear the axle housing.

4. Remove the speedometer drive cable from the right side of the torque tube by unscrewing the cable retainer.

5. Remove the cotter pins from the six castle nuts around the universal joint housing half-caps. Remove the six 3/8 inch nuts and bolts joining the caps to the center frame crossmember. Remove the two 3/8 inch, bolts and lockwashers holding the two u-joint half-caps together and remove the caps. Roll the rear axle out from under the truck, supporting the front of the driveshaft. Remove the wheels and place the rear axle assembly on a stand or the floor for disassembly. A hoist will probably be required to raise the assembly from the floor as it weighs over 450 pounds.

Disassembly (Bevel gear axle)

1. Remove the rear brake drums with a suitable puller or by hand if the brakes are backed off and the drum is loose. Remove the brake assemblies and backing plates as described in the brake chapter of this supplement. Remove the lock ring from the inside of the torque tube and slide the speedometer driving gear off of the shaft followed by the spacer and roller bearing assembly.

2. Cut the safety wire and remove the six bolts securing the torque tube to the differential housing. Remove the large nut and bolt securing the radius rods in front if they have not already been removed and slide the torque tube from the drive shaft.

3. Remove the eleven bolts, nuts and washers from the axle housing and pull the left side axle housing off of the axle shaft. Pull the axles, ring gear and differential carrier assembly out of the axle housing and lay it aside. Remove the radius rods from the left and right axle housings.

4. Remove the large rivet and separate the pinion drive gear from the driveshaft collar. With a large pipe wrench or adjustable wrench, remove the lock nut, nut locking plate and adjusting nut from the pinionshaft and pull the front pinion bearing out of the front of the right axle housing.

5. Cut the safety wire and remove the eight 7/16-14 hex head screws holding the two halves of the differential carrier together. Before separating the carrier sections, mark them with a punch or scribe so that they can be reassembled in the same position. These two are machined to match and must be replaced the very same way they come out. When these two parts are separated, the spider and spider gears will fall out. You will notice here that the AA-4211-B spider has four gear shafts rather than the three found in the Model A Car assembly. It is also larger of course. The carrier, axle shafts and ring gear may be separated and laid aside for inspection.

6. The AA-4609 driving gear and bearing race assembly do not separate as do the parts in the Model A car so they are serviced as a unit. If replacing the differential carrier and gear or the pinion gear, remember to identify whether they are for the 6.6:1 or 5.14:1 ratio as the parts are not interchangeable.

Above - June 1931 rear axle reinforcements are visible on either side of the housing.

Below - Inside of rear hub and drum showing BB-1225 wheelbearings and AA-1175-B grease retainer in place.

21

Inside of AA-4010 axle housing showing copper plate that rides against side of ring gear.

Differential case separated to remove spider and pinion gears.

Differential case, ring gear and axles of late 1931 AA rear axle assembly removed from housing.

Spider and pinion gear assembly.

Differential and ring gear assembly showing AA-4221-B differential cone and bearing assembly.

AA-4211 spider and AA-4215 pinion gears dissassembled.

Disassembly (Worm gear type)

1. Remove the brake drums with a suitable puller or by hand if the brakes are backed off and the drum is loose. Remove the brake assemblies and backing plates as described in the brake chapter of this supplement. Remove the lock ring from the inside of the torque tube and slide the speedometer driving gear off the shaft followed by the spacer and roller bearing assembly.

2. Cut the safety wire and remove the six bolts and nuts securing the torque tube to the differential housing. Remove the large nut and bolt securing the radius rods in front if they have not already been removed and slide the torque tube from the drive shaft.

3. Remove the four bolts from the AA-4190-R rear axle housing cap and remove the cap and gasket.

4. Remove the cotter pins and remove the thirteen bolts, and nuts from the axle housing and pull the AA-4014 axle housings off of the axle shaft. Note that these housings are identical. The AA-4610 worm gear will fall free from the assembly so be careful it is not damaged. The axle housings may be separated without removing the driveshaft if necessary due to the worm gear not being attached to either half of the axle housing.

5. Remove the eight cotter pins, bolts and nuts and separate the two halves of the AA-4205-AR differential gear case. You may now pull the axle shafts, differential gear, spider and pinions from the housing. Note that the Rear axle housing cap, differential gear case, pinions, spider and differential gear are the same as the corresponding parts for a TT truck. Notice also, that the spider has four pinion gears rather then three as does the Model car. The differential gear case is not different for the different gear ratios like the one is for the later bevel gear rear axle, so if the gears are to be replaced, you will only need to be aware of whether the worm and gear are 5.17:1 or 7.25:1 ratio.

Removal of AA-2600/2601 emergency brake carrier assembly.

AA-4610-AR worm for 7.25:1 rear axle.

AA-2211 rear brake housing with brake shoes removed.

Differential, 7.25:1 worm gear and axle assembly showing AA-4221-AR cone and bearing assembly.

Separation of halves of AA-4014-BR rear axle housing.

Axle assembly separated.

Inside of axle housing.

Axles, worm gear, spider and pinion gears.

24

Inspection and restoration

Inspection and restoration follows the identical procedures described in the car shop manual. New bearings, seals and races should be available from any good bearing supplier using either the original numbers or they may be ordered in most cases by taking the bearings to the dealer and having them duplicate the specifications or measure the widths and diameters yourself and have the specifications duplicated.

Before reassembly, remember to clean all parts of grease and rust and paint the outer housings with a semi-gloss black enamel.

Reassembly of the rear axle

Reassemble the rear axle in the reverse order of disassembly, paying close attention to the adjustments described on page 413 of the January, 1930 Ford Service Bulletins. Additional information concerning the assembly of the rear axle will be found on pages 545, 556-57, 564 and 576 of the 1931 Service Bulletins.

Torque tube assembly

The Ford AA truck was equipped with four different torque tube designs. The first was the unit in the 1928 to late 1992 trucks which was the AA-4505-BR. It was similar in design to the unit used on the Model A cars of the same period. It utilized the AA-4605-AR driveshaft.

The second design was the AA-4505-C used with the seldom seem 1928-29 bevel gear rear axle. This was used with the AA-4209-A and B driveshaft and driving gear assemblies. Illustrations of these parts may be found in appropriate editions of the Parts Price List.

The third was the AA-4505-F which was introduced with the 1930-31 style bevel gear rear axle. This first design had a slight visible shoulder toward the front of the housing. The later design BB-4505 tapered straight along its length and was used in the later 1931 Trucks. The AA-4505-F and BB-4505 are interchangeable. These units were both used with the AA-4605-G driveshaft.

Coupling shaft

There were four different coupling shaft and housing assemblies used on the AA truck. The first was the AA-4802-B used with the 1928 to late 1931-131 1/2 inch wheelbase chassis.

The other coupling shaft and housing assembly was the one used with the 157 inch wheelbase chassis. This is the AA-4802-C.

A later 1931-32 version of each of these units was equipped with a front universal joint assembly to facilitate removal of the transmsission without removing the rear axle assembly. I cannot find the part numbers for this unit but I have identified it on chassis AA4848011 which was a government mail truck. I do not know at what point this unit became available. It may have used a BB part number but it is a legitimate AA part because it requires the installation of the rear bearing retainer AA-7085-B illustrated elsewhere in this section.

AA-4505-F torque tube from March, 1931 truck with visible shoulder toward front. Notice two grease fittings at front of housing.

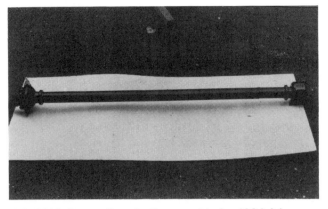

AA-4802-C coupling shaft assembly for 1931 AA-157 chassis.

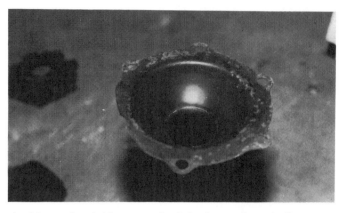

Inside and outside rear of original coupling shaft housing was painted what appeared to be Rock Moss Green.

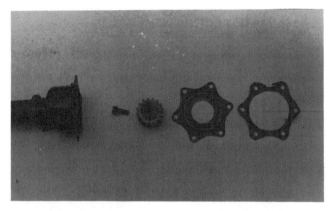

AA-4804-C coupling shaft housing, AA-4811 coupling shaft male gear, AA-7095 coupling shaft male gear retainer and gasket.

Front of AA-4802-C coupling shaft housing. Notice grease fitting. This part attaches to the rear of the transmission case.

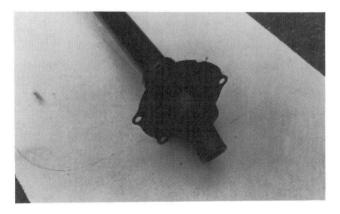

Assembled rear of coupling shaft and AA-7090-B universal joint for AA-157 chassis.

View from the rear of universal joint and coupling shaft installed in 1931 AA-157 chassis.

Unusual coupling shaft assembly found on 131 inch chassis AA4848011, which was a U.S. Mail truck. This shaft has a universal joint at both ends.

Parts of the coupling shaft disassembled. I cannot find numbers for this assembly in any A/AA parts book although it might be a BB-4803-A.

Front universal joint is different from the rear unit.

Rear of coupling shaft showing rear universal joint.

A heavy spring fits over the shaft inside the housing.

Unusual AA-7085-B rear bearing retainer used with this coupling shaft. It is similar to, but not the same as the retainer used to attach a four speed transmission to a Model A chassis

AA Service Letter Notes

August 16, 1928

We are using a Gurney angular type worm thrust bearing AA-4696A2 in the AA truck axle in place of the former type thrust bearing. This bearing operates more efficiently and will carry considerably more load. In every case, whenever necessary to disassemble an AA axle, be sure that these type bearings are installed.

November 22, 1928

We now have a grease retainer which is being installed in the AA truck axles just ahead of the worm. This retainer is of similar design to those used in the axle housings at the wheels and will prevent lubricant from being forced out of the axle and forward into the torque tube. The felt retainer A-22435-R has been removed and discarded and the new bearing retainer AA-4622-R is considerably thicker than the old AA-22437

On any truck axles which you overhaul, it is necessary to insert the parts AA-4700-R and AA-4622-R making certain that the edge of the retainer leather faces the worm roller bearing and retainer AA-4622-R is placed next to the bearing and the AA-4700-R is placed next to the retainer.

April 10, 1929

We are now using in production a redesigned AA-4696A2 Gurney thrust bearing in the AA worm gear axles. This bearing differs from ther previous type in that the retainer is heavier and has a wider surface resting against the thrust cap. In addition to this the surface of the thrust cap against which the bearing seats has been redesigned so as to eliminate the possibility of the bearing cutting a groove in the cap.

August 8, 1929

All AA-4696A2 old style Gurney thrust bearings which dealers have in stock should be returned to the branch for credit. Dealers should replenish their stock with the present type bearings which are 9-ball Gurney and 10-ball Federal, which are carried under the same number as mentioned above.

August 18, 1930

At present, the high speed axles are being shipped marked in two ways. Some are stamped 7-36 at the bottom right hand housing and others have a white metal tag attached stamped 7.36. The tag is assembled on the rear housing bolt. Both methods are optional. Low speed axles are readily identified as they are not atamped or tagged.

November 26, 1930

AA-4005-J, Rear axle assembly, low speed, AA-4005-K, Rear axle assembly, high speed, AA-4010-F Rear axle housing, right hand, AA-4011-D, Rear axle housing, left hand.

To provide bearing surface for the entire length of rollers of bearing AA-1225-C and thus prevent the possibility of them breaking, the chamfer at the end of the above housings has been changed from a 30 degree taper with a 3/8 inch radius to a 3/32" x 1/16" radius. The heat treatment has also been changed to insure proper hardness the full length of the bearing. Housings with this change are now being used in production in all AA units.

AA-4815-B Coupling shaft assembly for 131" truck, AA-4815-C Coupl;ing shaft assembly for 157" truck.

To maintain concentricity and reduce whip of the coupling shaft, the material has been changed from a hot rolled to a cold rolled steel. It is also specified that the run-out must not exceed .010". Also, the heat treatment in the gear end of the shaft has been changed to make for the longer wear of the gears. The diameter of the AA-4815-C has been changed from 1-5/16" to 1-7/16", whereas the inside diameters of parts AA-4804-B and C, Coupling shaft housing assemblies for 131" and 157" wheelbase trucks respectively has been changed to 1-9/16" and 1-19/32" instead of 1-9/16" to insure clearance with 1-7/16" diameter shaft on 157" wheelbase trucks. However, the diameter of the coupling shaft assembly on the 131" wheelbase truck has not been changed.

April 3, 1931

To eliminate complaints of whipping of the coupling shaft, we outlined in recent letters the use of the 7/16" diameter coupling shaft and the new universal joint. In addition, it is essential when replacing these parts for service, that the roller bearing surface on the end of the drive shaft be checked for wear, and if it is worn more than .005" under the production limits, which are 1.246/1.247", the drive shaft must also be replaced.

September 1, 1931

To provide greater strength in the universal joint assembly the distance across the opening at the center of the spider has been decreased approximately 1/8" leaving a notch at each trunnion for angular movement of the knuckles. Parts affected by this change are AA-4802-B, Coupling shaft assembly 131", AA-4802-C, Coupliong shaft assembly 157", AA-7090-B2, Universal joint assembly, AA-7064, Universal joint spider, bushing and ring assembly in carton.

The total gear reduction ratio between the engine and the rear wheels with the 5.14 to 1 and 6.6 to 1 ratios is as follows:

Ratio	5.14 to 1	6.6 to 1
High	5.14 to 1	6.6 to 1
Third	8.67 to 1	11.15 to 1
Second	15.89 to 1	20.39 to 1
Low	32.89 to 1	42.24 to 1
Reverse	40.19 to 1	51.61 to 1

The increase in speed of the truck, at the same number of engine revolutions, with the 5.14 to 1 gear over the 6.6 to 1 gear is slightly more than 28 per cent.

The miles per hour of the truck with the 5.14 to 1 and 6.6 to 1 rear axle at various engine speeds is as follows:

Engine RPM	Truck MPH: 5.14 to 1	Truck MPH: 6.6 to 1
600	10.7	8.5
1000	17.8	14.
1400	25.	19.5
1800	32.2	25.
2200	39.3	30.5
2600	46.5	36.
3000	53.6	41.5

SUPPLEMENT TO
Chapter 6

THE FRAME

THE AA truck, encompassing many variations, needed six different frames to satisfy every need of the truck customer. All of the frame designs utilized a 7/32 inch thick side member that 2 3/4 inches wide. The 131 1/2 inch and early 157 inch wheelbase frames were 6 inches deep at the deepest point. The later 157 inch wheelbase frames were 7 inches deep.

The first frame variation was the AA-5005-AR frame used on the early trucks. This frame was used in the 131 1/2 inch wheelbase length only. The front crossmember had the solid front engine mount and at the rear of the frame, a crossmember with an arch similar to the one used on the A car frame was found. The next version of the AA frame, introduced for the 1930 model year, was the AA-5005-B, which was 171 5/16 inches long.

In April of 1931, the 171 5/16 inch frame was discontinued and replaced with two variations, a short AA-5005-B for dump trucks that was 169 13/16 inches long, and a long version AA-5005-D that was lengthened to 181 5/16 inches.

For the 157 inch wheelbase truck, introduced in mid 1930, there were at least two variations, both 210 3/8 inch in length. The first was the AA-5006-AR, which was the tapered version made wider at the rear than at the front. The second version, introduced in January of 1931, was the AA-5008 with sides that remained parallel from a point just behind the cab.

In addition to those major changes in truck frames, there were many small changes that may be found in the Model A Service Bulletins. There were also differences in the spring hangers mounting the rear springs to the frame. They were made in a longer version in April of 1931 for the purpose of lowering the loading height of some trucks. These are described in the service bulletins. The 157 inch frame was the last Model to do away with the solid front engine mount, replacing it in January of 1931. Apparently, this mount was retained to add more strength to the front of the chassis on the long wheelbase model.

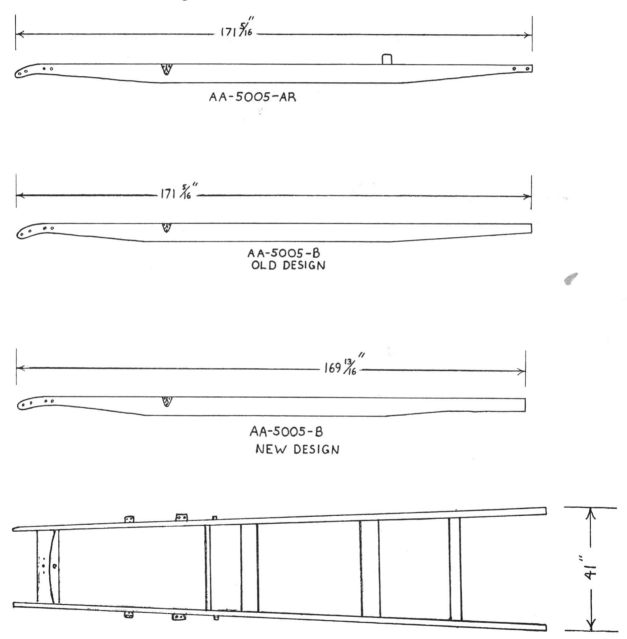

AA-5005-AR

AA-5005-B
OLD DESIGN

AA-5005-B
NEW DESIGN

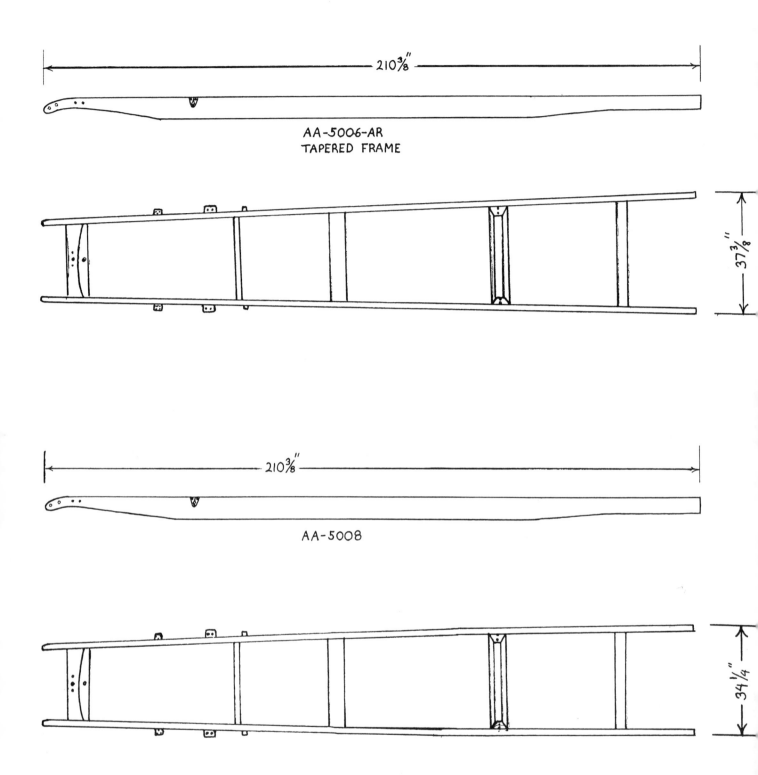

210⅜"

AA-5006-AR
TAPERED FRAME

37⅜"

210⅜"

AA-5008

34¼"

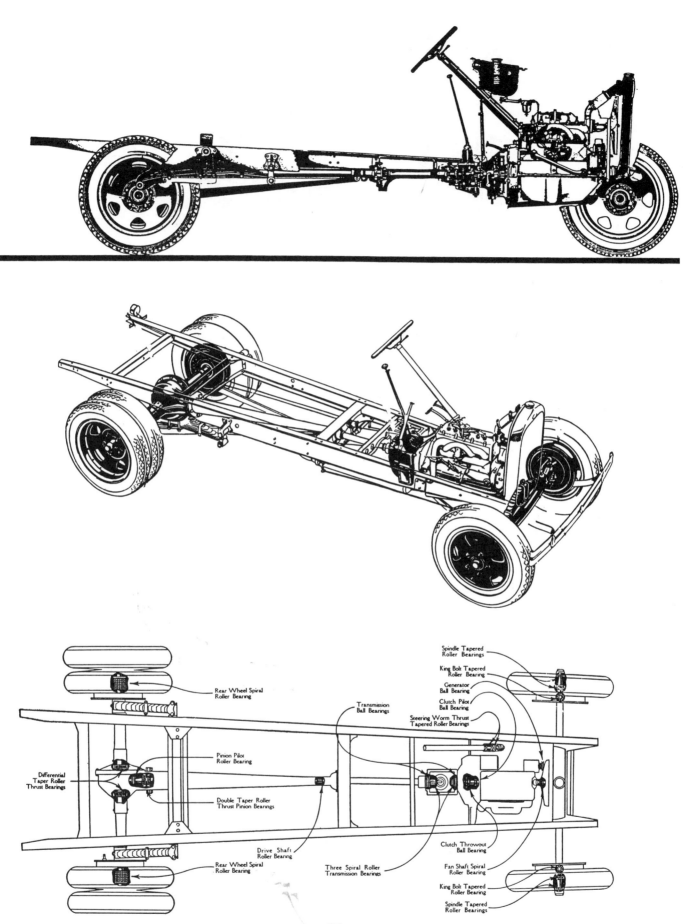

Spindle Tapered Roller Bearings

King Bolt Tapered Roller Bearing

Generator Ball Bearing

Clutch Pilot Ball Bearing

Steering Worm Thrust Tapered Roller Bearings

Transmission Ball Bearings

Rear Wheel Spiral Roller Bearing

Pinion Pilot Roller Bearing

Differential Taper Roller Thrust Bearings

Double Taper Roller Thrust Pinion Bearings

Drive Shaft Roller Bearing

Rear Wheel Spiral Roller Bearing

Three Spiral Roller Transmission Bearings

Clutch Throwout Ball Bearing

Fan Shaft Spiral Roller Bearing

King Bolt Tapered Roller Bearing

Spindle Tapered Roller Bearings

33

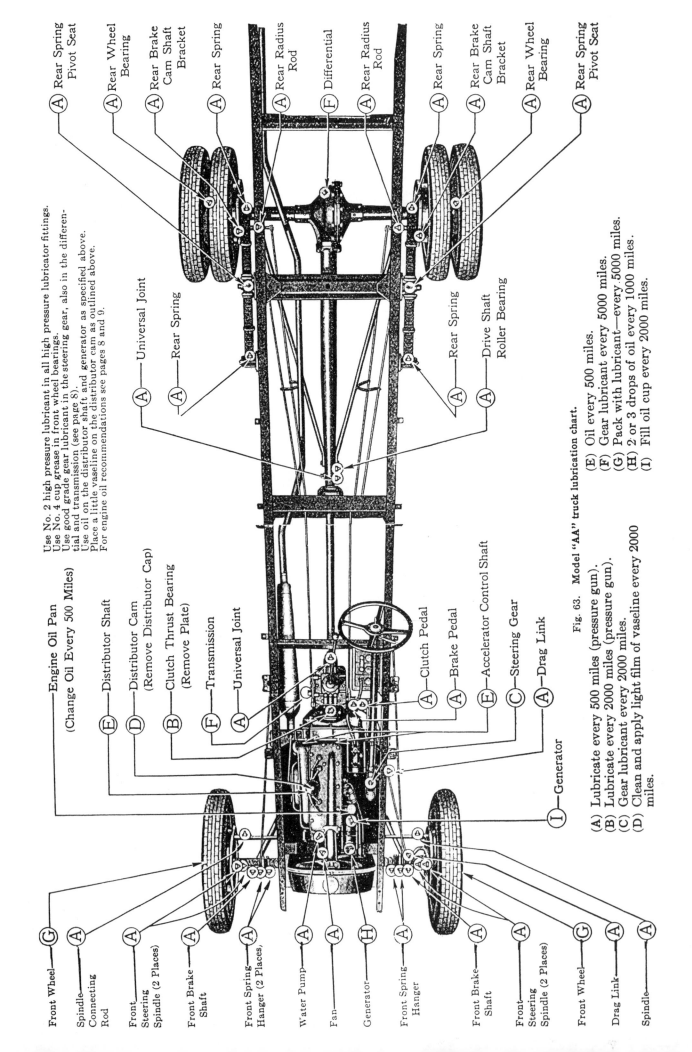

Ⓖ—Front Wheel

Ⓐ—Spindle
Connecting
Rod

Ⓐ—Front
Steering
Spindle (2 Places)

Ⓐ—Front Brake
Shaft

Ⓐ—Front Spring
Hanger (2 Places)

Ⓐ—Water Pump

Ⓐ—Fan

Ⓗ—Generator

Ⓐ—Front Spring
Hanger

Ⓐ—Front Brake
Shaft

Ⓐ—Front
Steering
Spindle (2 Places)

Ⓖ—Front Wheel

Ⓐ—Drag Link

Ⓐ—Spindle

Ⓔ—Engine Oil Pan
(Change Oil Every 500 Miles)

Ⓔ—Distributor Shaft

Ⓓ—Distributor Cam
(Remove Distributor Cap)

Ⓑ—Clutch Thrust Bearing
(Remove Plate)

Ⓕ—Transmission

Ⓐ—Universal Joint

Ⓐ—Clutch Pedal

Ⓐ—Brake Pedal

Ⓔ—Accelerator Control Shaft

Ⓒ—Steering Gear

Ⓐ—Drag Link

Ⓘ—Generator

Ⓐ—Rear Spring
Pivot Seat

Ⓐ—Rear Wheel
Bearing

Ⓐ—Rear Brake
Cam Shaft
Bracket

Ⓐ—Rear Spring

Ⓐ—Rear Radius
Rod

Ⓕ—Differential

Ⓐ—Rear Radius
Rod

Ⓐ—Rear Spring

Ⓐ—Rear Brake
Cam Shaft
Bracket

Ⓐ—Rear Wheel
Bearing

Ⓐ—Rear Spring
Pivot Seat

Ⓐ—Universal Joint

Ⓐ—Rear Spring

Ⓐ—Rear Spring

Ⓐ—Drive Shaft
Roller Bearing

Use No. 2 high pressure lubricant in all high pressure lubricator fittings.
Use No. 4 cup grease in front wheel bearings.
Use good grade gear lubricant in the steering gear, also in the differential and transmission (see page 8).
Use oil on the distributor shaft and generator as specified above.
Place a little vaseline on the distributor cam as outlined above.
For engine oil recommendations see pages 8 and 9.

Fig. 63. Model "AA" truck lubrication chart.

(A) Lubricate every 500 miles (pressure gun).
(B) Lubricate every 2000 miles (pressure gun).
(C) Gear lubricant every 2000 miles.
(D) Clean and apply light film of vaseline every 2000 miles.

(E) Oil every 500 miles.
(F) Gear lubricant every 5000 miles.
(G) Pack with lubricant—every 5000 miles.
(H) 2 or 3 drops of oil every 1000 miles.
(I) Fill oil cup every 2000 miles.

35

Inspection of the frame

The first step in inspection of the frame is to check for strightness and alignment of the rails and crossmembers. This is accomplished by measuring the frame diagonally with a tape measure and comparing the measurements.

The most difficult damage to identify is vertical twisting of the frame members. The best way to determine this is to place the frame on a level floor supported by evenly sized jack stands or blocks and measure the distance to the floor from side to side.

If there appears to be an excessive amount of deflection in the frame members it will be impossible to get a good body fit or a good front end alignment. Any variance of more than 1/8 inch in any direction should be considered excessive and steps should be taken to correct it. Any automobile or truck frame or body shop should have the equipment necessary to to straighten the AA frame, but if a shop of this kind is not available a frame may be straightened in the home shop with the use of a Porta-Power or hydraulic jack and heavy beams of wood or steel. If the damage is severe, a better choice would be to find another frame, although for a truck, frames are a little more difficult to find than for a car. Make sure that the new frame is one that matches the year of the truck being built.

Another area of inspection of great importance is the rivets mounting the crossmembers and brackets to the frame rails. If these rivets are loose or missing, they will need to be replaced with new rivets. Rivets are available from various suppliers, but they are better installed professionally with the proper equipment and skills. Some restorers like to replace the rivets in many parts with bolts. With trucks, I have found some of them may have been repaired this way years ago. If this method is chosen, be certain that the bolts are grade five or six hardened bolts and that they fit very tightly in the holes. It is probably best to drill the holes to fit the bolts.

Do not for any reason weld the frame members together. The frame and body structures on old cars and trucks were riveted so that there would be a certain amount of flexibility and movement between the parts. If these structures are welded,

they will not not give and the frame will creak and groan at every turn, in addition to causing damage to the body mounts and framework.

See the frame section of the Model A Shop Manual, pages 73-74 for steps in completeing frame restoration

AA-157 chassis on a March, 1931 truck. Notice the parallel frame rails behind the center crossmember.

Springs

The front springs for AA trucks included at least four varieties. The 1928-29 truck had a standard AA-5310-AR spring along with the heavier 18 leaf AA-5310-BR. These springs were the same width as the Model A car spring but with different rates and number of leaves.

When the heavier chassis was introduced in 1930, the AA-5310-C spring with 13 leaves became the standard unit. The 157 inch wheelbase truck was equipped with a 14 leaf AA-5310-D spring. This spring was also available on the 131 1/2 inch wheelbase chassis as an option for heavy duty use. Both of these springs are wider than the Model A car front spring and are in fact, the same width as a car rear spring.

The rear springs on all AA trucks were of the cantilever design. The rear of the spring is attached to a bearing surface on the axle housing and is able to rotate slightly with the axle movement.

The front of the spring is attached to the frame side rail with a AA-5775-A shackle bracket on each side. The center of the spring is attached to a pivot point on the frame with a AA-5785-B pivot bracket. Because the rear spring frame mount is in front of the axle housing, the cantilever design allows for the rear of the truck frame to be shortened if necessary for the installation of special dump bodies or other equipment. This type of design was used on the rear of some automobiles such as the Bugatti Royale Type 41.

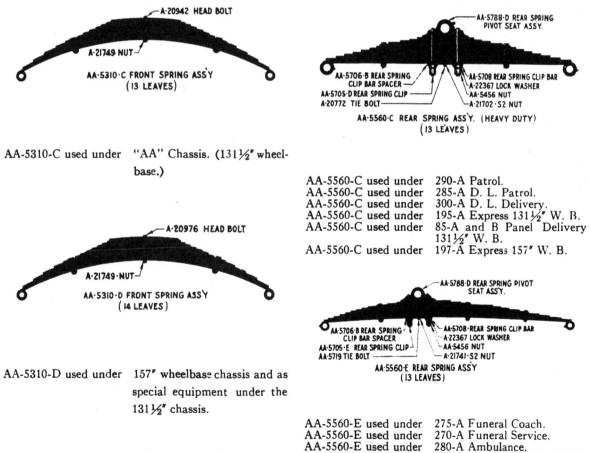

AA-5310-C used under   "AA" Chassis. (131½″ wheelbase.)

AA-5310-D used under   157″ wheelbase chassis and as special equipment under the 131½″ chassis.

AA-5560-C used under   290-A Patrol.
AA-5560-C used under   285-A D. L. Patrol.
AA-5560-C used under   300-A D. L. Delivery.
AA-5560-C used under   195-A Express 131½″ W. B.
AA-5560-C used under   85-A and B Panel Delivery 131½″ W. B.
AA-5560-C used under   197-A Express 157′ W. B.

AA-5560-E used under   275-A Funeral Coach.
AA-5560-E used under   270-A Funeral Service.
AA-5560-E used under   280-A Ambulance.
AA-5560E   special equipment under bodies 85-B, 290-A- '285-A, 300-A.

37

Spring restoration

The springs are restored in the same manner as the ones for the car. Because they are much heavier and thicker, they will generally not have as much wear showing as pasenger car springs. New bushings and shafts for rear springs are generally not available and any replacement bushings will have to be made either by using existing bushings from another application, or by making them from brass. A good machine shop can perform this service if necessary. Check with a local spring shop and they may be able to provide new bushings.

For the front end, the early trucks will use the same front spring hanger and bushing as the car. The later heavy duty front spring will use the same hanger and bushings as the rear spring on the passenger car. See the Ford Service Bulletins for more spring information.

Muffler and tailpipe

See page 558 of the April 1931 Ford service bulletins for information on the 1931 muffler and tailpipe variations. Any of these may be made by welding a new tailpipe to the cut-off end of a stock car muffler assembly. The earlier model trucks had the same muffler and tailpipe as the car chassis. This section also illustrates the special brackets required. The appropriate Parts Price list also gives more information on the lengths and application of the various tailpipe assemblies.

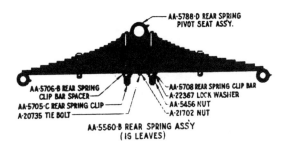

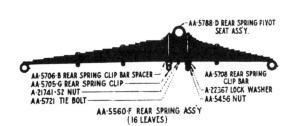

AA-5560-F used under   330-A School Bus.

NOTE: Truck rear springs as supplied through service include only one spring clip. The spring seat and the second spring clip are not included.

AA-5560-B used under   76-B Open Cab.

AA-5560-B used under   82-B Closed Cab.

AA-5560-B used under   185-B Platform 157″ W. B.

AA-5560-B used under   210-A Panel Delivery.

AA-5560-B used under   229-A Service Car.

AA-5560-B used under   187-A Platform 131½″ W. B.

AA-5560-B used under   242-A Express H. D. 131½″ W. B.

AA-5560-B used under   199-A Ice Wagon.   All dump bodies except 205-A.

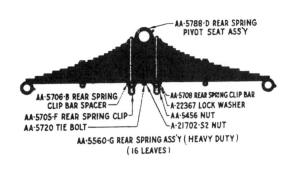

AA-5560-G   Heavy duty spring used under 205-A Hi-lift dump trucks and as special equipment under "AA" chassis.

AA Service Letter Notes

September 10, 1929

We are now in a position to furnish the AA-5310-B, 18 leaf front spring assembly to be used on trucks engaged in heavy duty work. When ordering these, it will also be necessary to include two AA-5455-C, Front spring clips.

April 8, 1930

The AA-5461, Starting crank bearings have been increased 1/2 inch in width(from 2" to 2-1/2") beneath the spring clip grooves to give more support for the spring clips. This does not affect the AA-5455, Spring clip now in effect.

July 15, 1930

AA-1468, Spare wheel carrier rear hinge bolt and nut assembly is a new part assembly for use on the platform body on the 157" chassis. This assembly isd the same as AA-1470-B except the hinge is 7" long rather than the 3-1/4" hinge on the AA-1470-B.

AA-1454, Spare wheel carrier assembly is a new number and part for use on the AA157 truck. The only difference in this carrier and the AA-1453-C is the AA-1468 bolt which is longer.

February 5, 1931

We are about to adopt a special wheel carrier of the fender well type to be mounted on the left side for use on various types of AA chassis; the following parts will be necessary to make this installation:

3-A-21223 Bolt
3-A-21893 Nut
3-A-23533 Washer(Wheel carrier support bracket to frame)
2-A-2163287 Nut
1-A-22139 Washer(Tire carrier support nut cover to wheel carrier flange), wheel carrier support to bracket
1-A-22306 Washer(Wheel carrier)
3-AA-1120-B Wheel carrier bolt nut
1-AA-1410 Wheel carrier support anti-rattler
1-AA-1416 Bracket
1-AA-1317 Wheel carrier support
1-AA-1423 Tire carrier support nut cover

1-AA-1431 Wheel carrier flange assembly
1-AA-16030 Front fender shield assembly LH
1-AA-16036 Front fender assembly with well LH
This type carrier is also adaptable to all late model trucks other than those on which they will be used as standard equipment.
(Author's note - There was also a later release of a AA-16035 right fender and shield with well that does not show up in any parts price list. This fender is illustrated elsewhere in this chapter.)

April 3, 1931

AA-5788-D, Rear spring pivot seat with bushing has been changed in that 1/16" has ben added to the bottom of the above part, changing the thickness of the flanges at the ends from 5/16" to 3/8" and thereby increasing the relief or offset in bottom of pivot seat, to allow more clearance for springs having high camber. The object of this change is to prevent the recoil forcing the top spring leaf against the top of relief in the pivot seat and causing the tie bolt head to shear.

Other changes made to conform to the above change have been made on AA-5705-C, Rear spring clip and AA-5705-D, Rear spring clip on which the lengths have been increased and the type of steel has been chnaged to prevent the clip from stretching. AA-5456, Rear spring clip is a new number and new design released to be used with the new style AA-5705-C & D. A-21895 has been obsoleted for this purpose. Parts A-20735 and A-20772, Rear spring tie bolts have ben changed in that the height of the head has been increased from 7/32-5/64" to 9/32-19/64" to allow the head to enter to the proper depth after increasing the depth of the relief in the pivot seat.

July 27, 1931

To avoid interference of the front end of the 48" long springs with the spare wheel carrier support brackets, when used on the AA Panel, Model 85B, the well fender and fender well type of wheel carrier must be used.

October 8, 1931

Wheel carrier assemblies for trucks without bodies are now released as standard equipment at no extra cost, effective at once. This means that we now supply a wheel carrier for all types of cars and trucks. Previous to this time trucks without bodies were supplied with the spare wheel bolted to the No. 5 crossmember. New style wheel carriers assemble under the chassis frame at the rear end. If you have any 131 1/2" wheelbase chassis on hand on which you desire to install this wheel carrier, we suggest that you follow these instructions. If the frame does not have the rivet holes punched in the No. 5 crossmember for the AA-1490 stop in the side members for the carrier hihges and hinge bolts, arrange to drill the necessary holes which are to be located as follows: Position the AA-1470-B hinge bolt and nut assembly on the left side member of the frame so that the upper hole measures 3-1/16" from the lower edges of channel and 21-19/32" to the rear of the front rivet which holds the No. 5 crossmember to the side member. All other holes for the carrier proper may be located by holding the wheel carrier assembly in position after the first hole is drilled. The spare wheel carrier stop on the side member of the frame is to be located 22-3/32" to the rear of the front rivet which holds the No. 5 crossmember to the side member. The spare wheel carrier stop on the No. 5 crossmember is to be located 2-3/8" to the right of the center line of the chassis.

The 157" wheelbase frame has all of the carrier holes punched.

The following are new parts specified to be used with the above operation:

AA-1479 Spare wheel carrier hinge block
AA-1490 Spare wheel stop front
1 each required for 131 1/2" wheelbase truck chassis without body.
1 each required for Model 85B Panel Delivery when AA-1451 carrier is used at the rear
AA-1451 Spare wheel carrier, now listed as standard equipment on 131 1/2" and 157" wheelbase truck chassis without bodies and listed as optional equipment with the side mounting on the 85B Panel Delivery Body.

December 9, 1931

To provide heavy enough rear springs for dump trucks to compensate for the possibility of overloading the 16 leaf heavy duty springs now being used on Model 205A, Coal body are specified for use on all dump trucks as standard equipment.

AA-5558-G Rear spring assembly 16 leaf(Heavy duty) 2 required on all dump, coal and garbage trucks.

AA-5558-A Rear spring assembly 16 leaf (short) 2 required on truck chassis except Models 85B, 270A, 290A, 300A, 195A, 197A, 275A, 330A and all dump coal and garbage bodies.

To provide more clearance for the muffler inlet pipe when used on the Standrive chassis, the size of the cutout on the A-5775, Engine pan has been increased.

AA-16035 right front fender with well and AA-16029 shield that are not shown in any Model A/AA parts list that I have seen. They appeared on a Government ordered U.S. Mail truck with a March, 1932 number.

AA-1417 Carrier Support, AA-1416 Bracket, AA-1418 Flange and AA-1423 cover for the fender mounted spare wheel. See page 528 of the January, 1931 Ford Service Bulletins for instructions on mounting.

SUPPLEMENT TO
Chapter 8

TRANSMISSION AND CLUTCH ASSEMBLY

THE early AA Ford truck is equipped with a standard car type three-speed transmission accompanied by an optional two-speed or dual-drive auxiliary transmission. The dual-drive is a planetary transmission operated by a foot pedal. The truck is equipped with a coupling shaft which connects the rear end of the transmission drive shaft and the universal joint. It is installed between the two center cross members of the chassis and is enclosed in a steel tube and supported by roller bearings at each end.

Installation of the coupling shaft was made specially to permit the use of a dual-drive. The dual-drive is connected behind the regular three-speed transmission.

The new four-speed selective gear transmission for the Ford truck was introduced in October of 1929. It was described as being of exceptionally heavy construction - large size gears and bearings being used throughout. All gears and shafts are made from special heat treated chrome alloy steel. The countershaft is carried on roller bearings. The roller bearing is also used at the front of the main shaft. Because of their effectiveness in carrying radial loads, the main drive gear and spline shaft are carried on ball bearings. This transmission was designed and built by Warner as a T8-1.

Operation of the dual-drive planetary transmission

The transmission is a constant mesh planetary type and gives 68% as much speed and 147% as much pulling capacity as the standard drive train. It applies in all speeds, giving the equivalent of six speeds forward. The illustration below shows the operating parts and installation of the dual drive transmission.

DUAL DRIVE

The standard Ford truck is equipped with a coupling shaft which connects the rear end of the transmission drive shaft and the universal joint. It is installed between the two center cross members of the chassis frame and is enclosed in a steel tube and supported by roller bearings at each end.

Installation of this coupling shaft in the standard truck was made specially to permit the use of a dual drive by truck users requiring special pulling power for their haulage units.

Removal of the shaft permits quick and easy installation of the dual drive between the two center cross members.

Transmission—Standard sliding selective gear type, three speeds forward, one reverse. Gears and shafts chrome alloy steel, heat treated for hardness. Main shafts in ball bearings, countershaft in roller bearings and reverse in bronze bushings.

Dual Transmission—Constant mesh planetary type. Gives 68 per cent as much speed and 147 per cent as much pulling capacity as standard truck. Applies on all gears, giving six speeds forward and two reverse. Optional at extra cost.

The dual drive is an auxiliary transmission connected behind the regular three-speed sliding gear transmission. It gives the truck six speeds forward and two reverse speeds. As a result, the driver has a slow, heavy pulling truck for heavy loads and poor roads, and a fast truck for less severe conditions.

This transmission is operated by foot controls projecting above the floor in easy reach of the driver's feet.

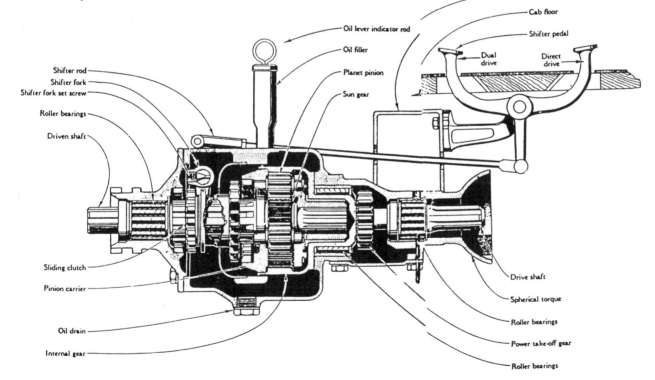

42

Operation of the four-speed transmission

In low speed the power comes in through the main drive gear into No. 1 countershaft gear, then through No. 4 countershaft gear into the large sliding gear on the main shaft and out to the coupling shaft.

In second speed the power comes in through the main drive gear into No. 1 countershaft gear, then through No. 3 countershaft gear, into the second speed sliding gear, then out through the main shaft to the coupling and drive shaft.

In third speed the power comes in through the main drive gear into No. 1 countershaft gear, then to No. 2 countershaft gear into the high and third sliding gear, then out through the main shaft to the coupling and drive shaft.

In fourth speed or high the power passes directly through the main drive gear and main shaft the same as the Model A car transmission.

In reverse, the power comes in through the main drive gear into No. 1 countershaft gear then through No. 4 countershaft gear into the reverse idler gear. From the reverse idler gear it goes into the low and second sliding gear, then through the main shaft to the coupling and drive shaft.

The illustration below shows the operation of the four-speed transmission.

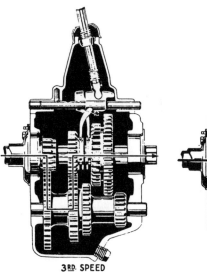

3RD. SPEED

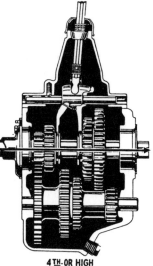

4TH. OR HIGH

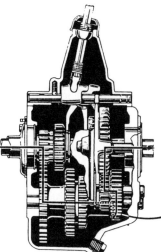

REVERSE

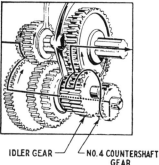

IDLER GEAR — NO. 4 COUNTERSHAFT GEAR

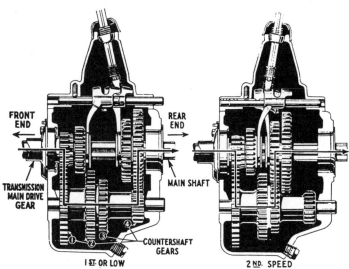

FRONT END — REAR END

TRANSMISSION MAIN DRIVE GEAR

MAIN SHAFT

① ② ③ ④ COUNTERSHAFT GEARS

1ST. OR LOW

2ND. SPEED

43

Transmission removal with engine previously removed from chassis

Removal is accomplished exactly the same as in the car except that this transmission assembly is much heavier and care should be taken when handling the unit.

Removal with engine in car

Removal is exactly the same as in the car except for the removal of the rear axle assembly. This process is covered in the rear axle chapter. Remember again that this transmission is extremely heavy and care must be used when handling it.

Basic transmission disassembly

1. Remove clutch inspection plate screws and plate from the clutch housing.
2. Remove the clutch bearing hub spring and slide the hub and bearing forward off sleeve.
3. Tap the old clutch release bearing off the hub and discard bearing.
4. Remove the four cap screws and lockwashers inside the clutch housing securing the housing to the transmission case. Carefully tap the housing to separate.
5. Remove the four 5/16 inch cap screws securing the clutch hub sleeve to the transmission and pull the sleeve off over the main drive gear shaft.
6. Using a soft brass rod, tap the main drive gear and bearing out through the front of the transmission case. Discard the mainshaft pilot bearing.
7. Carefully spread the main drive gear bearing retainer collar and slide it off the main drive gear.
8. Tap the main drive gear ball bearing off the gear using a soft iron or brass rod. Do not strike the bearing directly, as it hardened and could chip and cause injury. Discard the bearing but save the grease slinger washer and notice its position on the shaft.
9. Remove the Universal joint or AA-4811 coupling gear if not already removed by using a 9/16 inch socket to unscrew the cap screw securing the forward yoke or gear to the mainshaft. Engaging both sliding gears on the cluster gear will prevent the mainshaft from turning while removing the bolt.

10. Cut the wire securing the four 7/16 inch cap screws holding the rear bearing retainer to the case, and remove the cap screws and retainer.
11. Tap the mainshaft and bearing out of the rear of the transmission case using a soft mallet or rod. Slide the third and high gear (small) and low and second gear (large) from the mainshaft as the shaft is pulled out from the rear of the case.
12. Tap the mainshaft bearing off the mainshaft as in step 8. Discard the bearing and save the grease slinger washer.
13. Remove the 3/8 inch cap screw and retainer plate securing the reverse idler shaft and cluster shaft at the back of the transmission. Pull the reverse idler shaft out of the rear of the transmission case.
14. Tap the cluster gear shaft out of the front of the transmission case as the hole is reamed 0.0005 inch larger than the rear to reduce lubricant loss from the rear hole.
15. Remove the cluster gear and reverse idler gear.
16. Remove the cotter pin and drive the reverse shifter fork shaft out of the case and remove the shifter fork.
17. Drive out the pin and remove the AA-7510 clutch pedal shaft from the housing. Do not discard this shaft as you would with the car because it is different than the A-7510-C shaft and if it is worn, a new one will have to be made by a machinist. One of the pin holes on the truck shaft is drilled 10 degrees off center. This change is required for the clutch to operate properly.

(Top) Late 1929 AA-7006 transmission case. (Bottom) November, 1930 case. The WG stands for Warner Gear Co. Notice the pedal shaft.

The AA-7141 reverse Idler and power take-off gear. The power take-off gear and cover were made to an S.A.E. standard for all vehicles.

(Top)AA-7050 main drive gear bearing retainer. (Bottom) Front housing paper gasket in place.

Disassembly of transmission tower and shifter assembly

1. Remove the hand-brake assembly by removing two 7/16 inch cap screws on the side of the top cover.

2. Remove the cap from the early AA-7220-AR shifter cap by driving out the pin holding the cap and shifter lever. On the newer AA-7220-B design, unscrew the cap from the tower and remove the lever and spring. This change was made around November, 1930.

3. Remove the safety wire and lock nuts and drive the three shifter fork shafts and shifter forks from the housing. Notice the location and direction of the parts before removal. The shifter mesh lock and spring may be pried out of the way and then removed from the opening in the side of the housing when the plug is removed. Be careful of tapping too hard on the shafts and housing when trying to remove the shafts as the cast housing may be broken very easily. If the shafts are rusted into the housing, soak them first with a good penetrant such as Kroil, available from Kano Industries. You may also have to use a bit of heat to loosen the shafts on some trucks.

Clutch housing

The AA-7501 clutch housing is restored in exactly the same manner as described for the car on page 110 of the car shop manual. The only difference of course, is that the clutch pedal shaft is not part of the AA-7501 housing.

Cleaning and inspection

Cleaning and inspection of all components is performed the same as with the car units.

Transmission reassembly

1. Paint the exterior of all case parts Ford engine green except for the following parts, which should be painted gloss black: U-joint half-caps, clutch inspection cover, clutch release lever, clutch adjusting trunion and nut, clutch and brake pedals, and power take-off cover. All nuts, bolts, washers, screws, clevis pins and collars are plain or cadmium plated. For current finish acceptability, consult the MARC/MAFCA Judging Standards.

2. Assemble the reverse idler gear and shaft into the transmission case. The shifter fork groove should face the front of the case.

3. Assemble the two large roller bearings and spacer on the cluster gear. Lightly oil all of the bearings before assembly. Set the cluster gear in the transmission case. Set the transmission rear face down on a clean bench. Insert a long, narrow screwdriver into the cluster gear bore and align the gear with the case bore. Insert the cluster gear shaft from the front of the case.

4. Apply a light film of non-hardening brush-on gasket sealer to the cluster gear shaft rear bore in the case. Rotate the shaft so that the lock bar flat will face the reverse idler bore, and tap the shaft flush with the front face of the transmission case.

5. Apply a light film of gasket sealer on the end of the reverse idler shaft and press it in place and rotate it until the lock plate groove is flush with the rear of the case. Apply gasket sealer to the lockplate bolt threads, use a new lockwasher on the bolt and tighten it to approximately 15 foot-pounds using a 9/16 inch wrench. Check the gears for free spinning condition with a slight clearance or backlash.

6. Warm the front ball bearing by placing in on a 100 watt light bulb for ten to fifteen minutes. If the new replacement bearing is equipped with a snap ring, discard the ring. If the bearing is shielded, leave one shield in place but remove the shield on the side of the bearing facing the oil baffle. Place the bearing oil baffle over the main drive gear with the recessed center away from the gear.

7. Using insulated gloves, slide the warm ball bearing on the main drive gear with the oil baffle between the gear and the bearing.

8. Tap the bearing fully on the shaft using a soft iron or brass rod. The bearing outer race must not touch the oil baffle. If it touches, the baffle is bent or installed backwards. If the bearing is heated enough, it will go on without tapping and would be removable.

9. Slightly spread the main drive gear bearing retainer using snap-ring pliers and set in place on gear. Make sure that the retainer fits into the groove on the drive gear.

10. After the bearing has cooled, use a plastic-face mallet to tap the bearing into the front of the transmission case until the bearing stops against the retainer ring in the case.

11. Using four 5/16-18x3/4 inch cap screws and lock washers, secure the main drive gear bearing retainer to the front of the transmission case with a new gasket and gasket sealer. Be sure that the oil-return notch in the gasket is at the bottom to align with the hole in the case. Ensure that the clutch release bearing spring hole is at the top. Torque the retainer bolts to 10 foot-pounds.

12. Slide an oiled, short roller bearing into the bore on the inside of the main drive gear.

13. Assemble oil baffle to the rear side of the mainshaft and collar assembly with the recessed center away from the collar.

14. Warm and install the AA-7065 rear ball bearing in the same manner as the main drive gear bearing. Check the baffle for clearance with the outer race.

15. After the bearing has cooled start the mainshaft into the case, pilot bearing first. Slide the first and second (large) gear onto the splines of the mainshaft being certain that the collar portion of the gear for the shifter forks faces to the front of the transmission. Slide the third and high (small) gear onto the mainshaft, being sure that the collar

portion faces the rear. The collar portion of both gears should be adjacent to one another. Carefully slide the assembly into position in the transmission case. The pilot portion should slide easily into the main drive gear pilot roller bearing. The rear bearing may need careful tapping to seat it into the case.

16. Check the operation of all the gears at this time. See that the gears operate according to the description at the beginning of this chapter. All of the gears should operate with no scraping or binding.

17. If all positions check out correctly, apply gasket sealer to the rear bearing retainer AA-7085-B if a front universal joint is used. Install it with the grease fitting on the bottom and secure with four 7/16-20x1 inch drilled head cap screws and lockwashers. Torque to 35 foot-pounds. Safety wire these bolts making sure that the twisted wire ends are pushed close to the cap. If the truck is equipped with the more common type of coupling shaft drive gear, the retainer cannot be secured until the coupling shaft is installed and the unit is in the chassis. In this case, two gaskets and sealer will be used.

18. Place the universal joint or coupling shaft gear on the mainshaft splines. Secure the gear or U-joint with washer locating tab for the U-joint and 3/8-24x1 inch hex-head cap screw and new lockwasher. Torque to 22 foot-pounds. The basic transmission is now complete except for the installation of the top cover. This is best done after the unit is in the chassis

Transmission shifter and tower assembly

Assemble this part in the reverse order of disassembly.

Clutch housing assembly

Follow the same directions given in the car shop manual on page 117. The main difference will be in the size and number of the clutch housing to transmission bolts and lockwashers. The AA uses six 1/2-13x1 3/8 inch hex head bolts.

AA-7501 clutch housing assembly is easily distinguishable from its Model A counterpart.

Four-speed transmission assembly installed in 1931 AA-157 chassis. Notice that AA-7165 power take-off cover is painted gloss black.

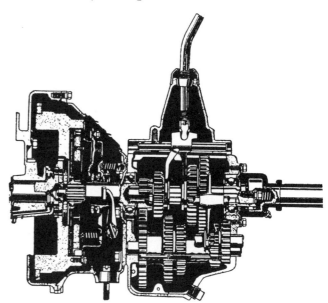

47

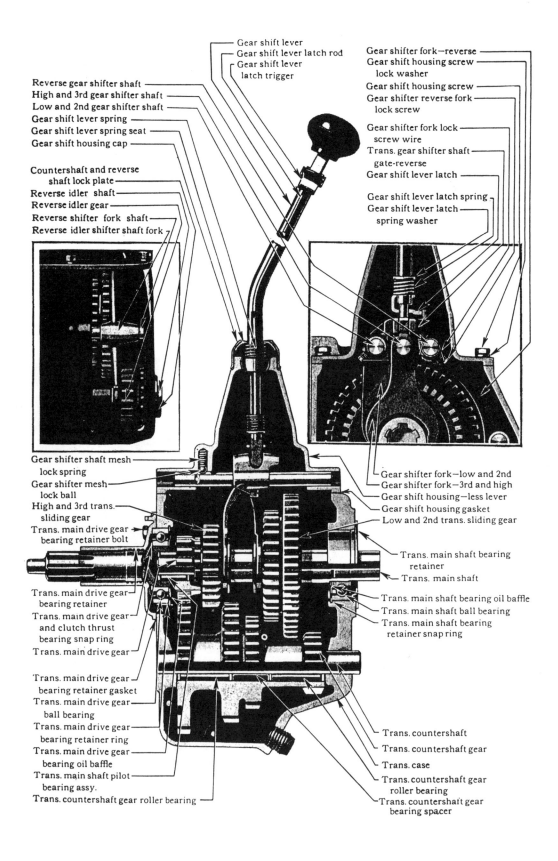

Gear shift lever
Gear shift lever latch rod
Gear shift lever latch trigger

Gear shifter fork—reverse
Gear shift housing screw lock washer
Gear shift housing screw
Gear shifter reverse fork lock screw
Gear shifter fork lock screw wire
Trans. gear shifter shaft gate-reverse
Gear shift lever latch
Gear shift lever latch spring
Gear shift lever latch spring washer

Reverse gear shifter shaft
High and 3rd gear shifter shaft
Low and 2nd gear shifter shaft
Gear shift lever spring
Gear shift lever spring seat
Gear shift housing cap

Countershaft and reverse shaft lock plate
Reverse idler shaft
Reverse idler gear
Reverse shifter fork shaft
Reverse idler shifter shaft fork

Gear shifter shaft mesh lock spring
Gear shifter mesh lock ball
High and 3rd trans. sliding gear
Trans. main drive gear bearing retainer bolt

Gear shifter fork—low and 2nd
Gear shifter fork—3rd and high
Gear shift housing—less lever
Gear shift housing gasket
Low and 2nd trans. sliding gear

Trans. main shaft bearing retainer
Trans. main shaft

Trans. main drive gear bearing retainer
Trans. main drive gear and clutch thrust bearing snap ring
Trans. main drive gear

Trans. main shaft bearing oil baffle
Trans. main shaft ball bearing
Trans. main shaft bearing retainer snap ring

Trans. main drive gear bearing retainer gasket
Trans. main drive gear ball bearing
Trans. main drive gear bearing retainer ring
Trans. main drive gear bearing oil baffle
Trans. main shaft pilot bearing assy.
Trans. countershaft gear roller bearing

Trans. countershaft
Trans. countershaft gear
Trans. case
Trans. countershaft gear roller bearing
Trans. countershaft gear bearing spacer

48

AA Service Letter Notes

August 16, 1928

We are now using solid roller type countershaft bearings AA-7120 and AA-7121 for use in all AA truck transmissions. Whenever it becomes necessary to replace a countershaft bearing, you will make certain that the solid roller type is used.

October 5, 1928

The Dual-high unit for trucks has been redesigned to improve the operation. This new design is interchangeable with the old design as a complete unit. Several of the components are slightly different. The lubricating specifications are also changed and it becomes necessary to use grease in place of oil; it will be satisfactory lubricate this unit with the same gear compound used in Model A differentials and transmissions.

Ocotber 9, 1930

To reduce the possibility of oil leakage, the gear shift lever cap will be screwed on to the transmission housing instead of being pinned on. This means that that gear shift housing will be threaded at the top of the tower and the gear shift lever cap will be threaded inside. The new numbers are as follows:
AA-7209-B Transmission gear shift lever assembly
AA-7221-B Gear shift lever trunnion
AA-7220-B Gear shift housing cap
AA-7222-B Gear shift housing

July 8, 1931

The four-speed transmission and clutch assembly has been made adaptable to the Model A chassis in order to provide a power take-off when desired. When installing the truck engine in the Model A chassis, it is only necessary to have a special universal joint, A-7090-C, Universal joint retainer, AA-7095, Transmission rear bearing retainer, A-7085-E and transmission rear bearing retainer screws, A-20866(six required). The four-speed transmission as you were advised in a special letter will be available through service for installation in any Model A chassis and will also be furnished as special equipment at extra cost if you desire it to be furnished in a new car on our final assembly line.

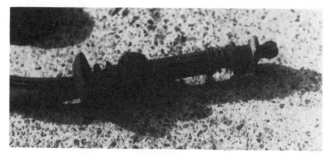
AA-7209-B shift lever with AA-7212 latch rod and spring attached. It is important that this end be restored to proper condition to work properly.

AA-2455 brake pedal is thicker and stronger than the Model A counterpart. The AA clutch pedal is the same A-7520 as used in the car chassis but it gets the AA-7523 clutch pedal spring.

This fabricated frame spreader may be necessary to install the clutch housing into the frame. It will work with the A or AA chassis.

49

SUPPLEMENT TO
Chapter 12

BODY AND FENDER ASSEMBLY

FORD truck bodies were varied in design and purpose according to the needs of the customer. The unusually broad selection of bodies made the Ford truck an exceptionally popular choice for truck buyers.

It was determined early in Model AA production that only 12 percent of the trucks being shipped from the factory had bodies. This meant that outside suppliers were making a great deal of money supplying bodies for Ford trucks. Charles Sorensen, in charge of production assigned Daniel Hutchins, head of truck sales, and Harold Meekin the task of setting up a truck department in each Ford branch and then training a man to call on Ford truck buyers to see what kind of bodies they wanted and to relay the specifications to Ford.

This led to Ford producing a body for just about every purpose imaginable. Eventually, the AA was offered in over 70 different body variations.

Although these bodies differed in many ways from those used on the Model A car, the construction methods were generally the same. Although the late 31 82B cab was one of the first all-steel bodies, but the rest of the line consisted of bodies built in the time honored composite wood and steel construction. Of course, when discussing AA trucks, the term "body" means the equipment on the back of the chassis, not just the cab. In some cases, the Ford truck was sold as a chassis cab so that the owner could purchase and install any body of his own choosing. A list of some of the builders supplying bodies for the AA truck may be found in the heavy commercial section of the MARC/MAFCA Judging Standards.

The illustrations at the back of this chapter show some of the bodies available on the AA.

General body information, body removal, service and fitting are identical to that of the Model A car and this information may be found in the car shop manual.

Because the original Model A shop manual does not have detailed information on body restoration, this information, adapted directly from the RESTORER'S CLASSIC CAR SHOP MANUAL, will be included here. All of it is also applicable to the Model A car and includes the latest in technology and materials.

Body restoration

Once the body is removed and disassembled, it should be placed on suitable sawhorses or a body platform and all parts should be cleaned of rust and paint. This may be accomplished by sand-blasting or by chemical dipping. If the body is to be sandblasted, be sure that the workman knows to be careful of warpage by not using excessive pressure. Although sandblasting leaves a rougher finish for better paint adhesion, some feel that dipping is better because the chemical solutions reach areas that cannot be reached by sandblasting. There are proponents of both methods and either one works well.

A new method only recently available is what is known as plastic media blasting. This process is now becoming available in many cities and provides a means of removing paint without damaging other parts of the body. This process is performed at low pressure and can remove paint from even small sections of the body that may only require partial repair. It will not remove rust or corrosion, but the quality of the metal after the old paint has been removed is extremely smooth and almost ready for finishing.

As soon as the body components are stripped of rust and paint, the bare metal should be treated with a metal prep solution and a good epoxy primer such as PPG DP 40 or duPont Variprime 615S should be applied to prevent any further rust. Do not use any metal prep materials that require a water wash as this defeats the purpose of cleaning to expose it to more moisture. DP 40 or Variprime primer seals the surface and where the undercoat is intact, the metal will not rust.

The next step to body restoration is the removal

of all dents, dings and distortions. It is important to get as smooth a metal surface as possible before any finish materials are applied. The less filler or lead that is required, the better the final product will be. Removing dents will require some good body hammers and dollys. Remember that a dent is stretched metal and the only way that this metal can be repaired is to shrink it back to its original size. This can be accomplished with a shrinking hammer and shrinking dolly or lead dolly. Another way to shrink metal is with a torch and shrinking hammer. All of the pounding in the world without proper shrinking technique is only going to stretch the metal more and work harden it so that it will be even more difficult to repair

A new method of shrinking metal is the shrinking disc available from Sunchaser Tools. This tool heats and shapes the metal at the same time to remove high spots easily. It is used with a body grinder such as a Milwaukee 6095. Finish the panels with a Vixen file and grinder until the surface is straight. Begin sanding with 40 and then scuff with 80 grit sandpaper. All sanding scratches should be removed with no coarser than 180 grit paper before any primer is applied. If this is not done, it will be difficult to keep the scratches from showing through the surface.

If there are any rusted out panels that need to be replaced, these will need to be repaired at this point. Since many replacement panels are available for the Model A and AA, there should not be too many newly fabricated panels that are required. If any are to be made, they may be made by a good body shop or the restorer may want to try this at home with some of the body shaping tools sold by The Eastwood Co. 18 gauge steel is a good thickness to use. If an English wheel is not available or there are no large sweeping panels to do, a soft hammer and sand bag will be required to beat out the shape. The skill to accomplish this takes lots of practice and experience.

There are varying methods for attaching the new panels to the old body. One of the best is the use of a MIG (Metallic Inert Gas) welder. A MIG welder, utilizing Argon and CO_2 will allow the panels to be fused without undue heat warpage. Some restorers like to use the butt weld, but a good job may be done using a lap weld if the panel is prepared properly. Spray the back side of the panel and the patch with DP 40 or Variprime to prevent rust forming under the weld at a later time. Be sure to cut the opening out far enough from the border of the rust damage to reduce the chance of the rust returning and damaging the finished body. Cut the new patch larger than the hole and in the same general shape.

Replacement corner and rear body panels and crossmember for a 1931 82-B body.

Sometimes the rust-out in this area will be so bad that additional filler is needed.

82-B corner patch panel spot-welded in place.

Corner brace is held in place with rivets but these may be replaced with small carriage bolts.

Carefully weld the new panel over the opening and if you can reach the backside, hammer the hot weld with a hammer and dolly to flatten it as much as possible. It is usually necessary to hammer the weld from the backside as the welding is being done to prevent the collapsing of the surface as it is heated. It is a good idea to hammer the weld with a wedge hammer. Welding may also be accomplished with an oxyacetelene welder with about a #2 tip. Try a setting of about 10 p.s.i. acytelene and 20 p.s.i. oxygen for sheet metal. Be sure to have a neutral flame. Finish the weld using the same methods as the MIG weld. When the weld is completed, the surface is ready for finishing.

There are some metal workers who can finish a hammer weld almost as smooth as the parent metal, but most will require some type of filler. Even though most modern plastic fillers can do a very good job, some restorers will still want to use lead.

The key to a good lead job that will not pop out is cleanliness of the metal. Before anything else, clean the metal surface with enamel reducer and let it air dry. Next, be sure that the surface is cleaned well with a good metal conditioner such as RM or duPont that does not require a water wash. Adding water to a surface defeats what we are trying to accomplish.

It is important that the surface be thoroughly tinned. Tinning means that you need to coat the surface with solder so that the body lead will stick. Tinning may be accomplished with acid core solder or tinning butter. Use a #4 tip with the torch and a soft flame using acetylene only. As the tinning solder is applied, move in one direction and wipe the surface with steel wool or cloth. Be sure that the entire area to be repaired is well coated with the solder before beginning the leading.

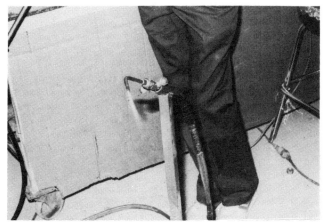

It is a good idea to make a stand to hold the welding torch when not in use.

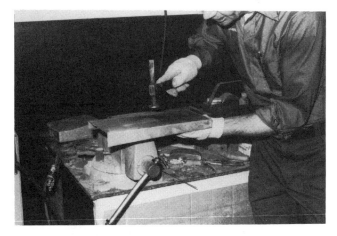

Hammer-welding skill may be developed with practice and patience.

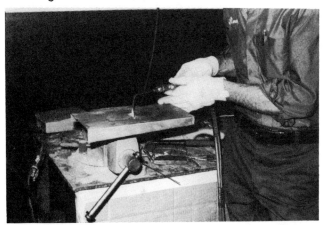

Tinning the metal first insures that the solder will adhere properly

53

A good layer of solder in place ready for finishing with files and sanding.

Use 70-30 body lead available from any auto body supply store or from Eastwood. Body lead comes in sticks which are melted carefully across the panel twisting the lead as you go. When sufficient lead is laid on the repair area, preheat the lead with a torch and spread it evenly with a wooden paddle lubed with tallow or wax. As you prewarm the lead and shape with the paddle, try to get the lead as close to the final shape of the panel as possible. When the leading is complete, wipe the area clean with enamel reducer to remove the tallow or wax. Always use a wax and grease remover before applying any finish to be sure that the surface is clean. It can never be too clean.

In some cases, the restorer will have a reason to use plastic filler instead of lead. There are some plastic fillers available today which work very well and are easier for the amateur to learn to use than lead. A good filler is Evercoat Tack Free, a light weight, easy to use filler that dries tack free in 15 minutes. It is very easy to work and sand. An important point to remember is that the application of plastic filler over bare metal will create a situation of heat and moisture that will make rusting begin almost immediately. Anytime a plastic filler is to be used, coat the entire panel with PPG DP 40 Epoxy primer to seal the surface. DP 40 or duPont Variprime will promote adhesion and prevent rust under the filler so that it will not fail later. Remember, we are building a vehicle to last as long as possible, not just get a job out the door as in a production body shop.

When the filler is applied and sanded, coat it with more DP 40 to draw the shrink out of the filler. Wait until the next day and sand again to assure a permanently smooth surface. If anytime during the finishing process, bare metal is exposed, the metal should be coated again with primer.

Priming

When all of the metal work is completed and the surface is as smooth as the final finish should be, the body is ready for primer. Actually, if we are taking a while with the body work, it may be a good idea to coat the entire body with a good non-water wash metal conditioner before going into the body work. This will help prevent rust from making things worse than when you first began. As the work is being completed, apply one good wet coat of DP 40 or Variprime primer to preserve and seal the surface against corrosion. Remember, from the time that the metal prep is applied, do not touch the body with hands or shop towels. Use only paper items such as Kimberly Clark Tough Cat towels. Shop towels may contain silicone and silicone is almost impossible to remove from the metal. Any contamination will prevent the finish from adhering properly. A good product to remove silicone if its presence is suspected is duPont Prep-Sol 3919. PPG DX 330 will not remove silicone.

Whether you are planning to use lacquer or some other finish for the final color, PPG K200/K201 or K 36 PRIMA primer-surfacers are recommended to top the DP 40 if a surfacer is needed. Remember, DP 40 should be topcoated within a week or it will need to be sprayed again. If it is left to sit too long it may become contaminated. Use a wax and grease remover again before the next coat of DP 40 or before the K200/K201.

K200 primer-surfacer is designed to fill in any small surface imperfections left from the body work or from the pits in the metal. Follow the directions on the can for best results. K200 primer-surfacer must be sanded for succeeding coats to adhere. Sand the primer-surfacer with a 320 or 360 wet or dry or waterproof paper until the surface is smooth. Apply more if necessary. It is a good idea to use a light mist guide coat of a different color primer to check your work. A spray can of lacquer primer will work well for this. The importance of using a guide coat cannot be overemphasized. Sand in as many different directions as possible to insure that you are not creating grooves in the surface. Remember to begin sanding from the level area that you want the repair to match. If you desire, you may want to use duPont URO Primer-Filler in place of PPG K200. The finishing steps are the same.

If there are any small imperfections remaining in the surface, fill them with Evercoat two part glazing putty. When the putty is dry, sand again with 80-180 and recoat with primer surfacer. Do not use lacquer spot putty such as PPG Red Cap.

This type of putty is nothing more than thick lacquer primer and will cause shrinkage problems later. Stay away from air dry materials as much as possible.

Because the K200/K201 primer-surfacer hardens so well, it is necessary for it to be sanded for the finish coats to adhere. K200 may be sanded the next day after spraying with no worry of shrinkage. If you are not sure that you sanded everywhere, use PPG DAS 1947 or 1980 sealer to promote adhesion. Spray one coat, wait 1/2 hour and spray another coat. This surface may now be finished with lacquer or with acrylic urethane such as PPG Deltron or duPont ChromaOne. The use of lacquer primer-surfacer is not recommended in any case as it will shrink for quite some time and cause problems later. Lacquer primer-surfacer probably causes more problems than it ever helps. Remember, lacquer was introduced to speed up production finishes in a factory or production body shop, it has no other redeeming qualities.

Fitting the body

The fitting of the body components and the body to the frame should be accomplished before the final paint is applied. If the body is fitted afterward, the trim or molding colors will not align and the paint may be scratched during the fitting process. The fit of the doors is very critical to the looks and enjoyment of any car or truck. It will certainly ruin a trip or tour if the door does not close or comes open while going down the road. The fit of the doors is also important to seal out rain and wind from the interior.

The doors are aligned with the body by use of shims under the body where it bolts to the frame. If the door is low at the latch side, raise it by placing shims under the bolt nearest the hinge of that door. Usually, rubber pads of 1/4 inch to 3/8 inch thickness work well as shims. Remember to pull the body bolts up tight each time the body and door fit is checked. Sometimes, the door problem can be traced to worn hinges and hinge pins. new pins and oversized pins are available, but the biggest problem is usually removing the old ones.

Hinge pins may be removed by using a large C-clamp. Place the clamp over the hinge pin with a small socket on top and the clamp pushing against the bottom of the pin. Tighten the clamp, and the pin should loosen enough to be driven out. You may want to apply a little heat or some good penetrating oil such as Kroil from Kano Laboratories to the hinge pin to assist in the loosening process. Be careful not to spread the bottom of the pin, or it will not come through without being sawed apart. Some pins are rusted in so tightly that the only way to get them out is to remove the entire hinge and drill the pin out on a drill press.

When the time comes to mount the body to the frame, webbing is usually placed between the frame and the body blocks or body framework. When the body and doors are properly mounted, the doors should close and latch easily without any twisting or forcing. It is important that the body be fitted and mounted properly before any top or upholstery work is done, or wrinkles will surely appear in the finished product.

Body finishing

A trick that may simplify the painting of the moldings and belt colors is to paint them first and then mask and apply the main body colors. Even though it was not usually done this way originally, it may be easier to mask the moldings than the entire body. Look at your particular body design and determine if this method may work for your truck. Remember that generally, AA trucks did not use molding colors although it is not incorrect to do so.

Although original finishes were of nitro-cellulose lacquer or pyroxylin as Ford called it, the modern restorer now has the choice of lacquer, enamel or acrylic urethane finishes. If the finishing is done properly, it will probably be impossible for anyone to tell the difference by looking at the vehicle. Because enamel is not generally recommended for use by the amateur painter due to its drying properties, only lacquer and acrylic urethane will be discussed here as body finish materials.

It is assumed at this point that the body has been properly prepared with metal prep, primer and primer-surfacer if necessary. The primer-surfacer should have been sanded and/or sealed and a careful inspection made of the finish to be sure that it is ready for the final color.

One of the things that usually takes a great deal of consideration in the restoration of any vehicle is the choice of color. For the early 1928-29 trucks, there are not many choices as the bodies were generally Rock Moss Green, Commercial Gray or Gunmetal Blue, the 1930-31 models offered a much greater selection of colors. By late 1931, the commercial Ford was available in 39 colors in any combination. Use the MARC/MAFCA Judging standards and select the color that is most pleasing to you. In some cases, you may want to finish the truck in a special commercial color that may have been used for a large company with a fleet order. This is one of the nice things about restoring a truck, you have more opportunity to personalize it.

There are dealers advertising in The Model A News, The Restorer and in Hemmings or other old car publications who offer original shades in lacquer if you wish. If you want more modern materials, many of these dealers will also mix the Model A Colors for you in acrylic urethane and in enamel for the wheels and frame. If you decide to use lacquer, PPG has formulas to mix most of the Model A colors. Some of the truck colors are not readily available at this time, but they may soon be as new information becomes available.

Painting the body (lacquer)

Acrylic lacquer will produce an excellent finish if applied carefully and patiently. The important thing to remember about lacquer is that it dries from the outside in. Each coat must be allowed to flash or dry thoroughly before the next coat is applied. This seems to be especially important with nitrocellulose material. If it is not allowed to dry at least 30 minutes between coats, it will not dry properly. Sometimes, the paint will still be wet the next day because the solvents on the first coats are soaking through the last coats.

The solvents in acrylic lacquer will also dissolve the lacquer underneath. Remember this when applying lacquer finishes so that you will understand the problems that may appear. One of the first mistakes that many painters make is to use a slow drying thinner such as PPG DTL 105. This thinner will give you a high gloss finish

needing very little rubbing out, but it will also cause sand scratches and swells to appear. This type of thinner dissolves the finish more because it takes longer to dry. Since you are going to be sanding and rubbing out the finish, it is not desirable to use a slow drying thinner. A medium thinner such as DTL 876 will do a better job.

Your equipment is another factor in a good finish. Use as good a quality paint gun as you can afford. A Binks Model 7 is a good choice for all around paint work. Even though the import copies look just like the Binks, the difference is in the amount of paint they put on and the even flow of the pattern.

Another choice today is one of various types of High Volume-Low Pressure systems available These new types of guns use various technology to allow more material to go on the body with less overspray. This not only cuts down on airborne pollution, but allows you to create a better quality finish. We will discuss this equipment in detail later in this chapter.

A compressor of at least two horsepower is usually required for automotive paint work. A smaller compressor will not be able to keep up with the volume of air needed to apply automotive finishes. Use a good inline filter at the gun and change it often to prevent moisture and dirt from getting in the finish. The use of a large filter such as a Motor Guard closer to the compressor will serve as added insurance. The Motor Guard uses toilet paper as a filter medium.

It is a good idea to purchase three to four gallons of color for the average vehicle. Shake, stir and mix all of the paint and pour it into a five gallon can. This will insure that all the differences in color mix are taken up. Pour all of the paint back into gallon cans. Keep one or two gallons to save for future repairs. Reduce three gallons of color 1 1/2 to 1 with the medium thinner. The paint will keep thinned as long as no air is allowed to enter the cans. With the extra paint, keep a note of the way the body was painted including the type of gun, air pressure, humidity, temperature, formula, thinner, and coats used. This information will help to match the finish exactly should the need ever arise. Mixing the paint with the thinner does not apply to the urethane and hardened enamel paints.

All spraying with a conventional gun should be done at 45 pounds pressure at the gun. Do not depend on the pressure indicated at the compressor as the length and size of the hose will lower the pressure. Be sure that the vent hole in the top of the paint gun is kept clean at all times. Try to do one panel at a time shutting off the gun at the end of each pass. Keep the gun parallel to the panel, do not tilt it. Overlap 50% on each pass on the panel. Six double coats should be the maximum amount of paint put on any car. The person who tells you he is putting twenty coats of lacquer on a car is telling you any of three things. One, he did not prepare the panel properly and is trying to fill defects with paint. Two, he is going to sand off most of that paint leveling the finish. Three, the twenty coat finish is invariably going to crack, check and fail at a later date because there is too much material on the car. Some people like to finish with two or three coats of clear. I recommend against using lacquer clear as it does not hold up well. If you must use clear, use Deltron DAU 82 or equivalent. Another trick that may increase the quality of the finish is to double the thinner in the final coat or two to achieve more flowout and gloss.

It is a good idea to wait at least two weeks before trying to sand and rub out the lacquer finish. If you did not have the good sense to use epoxy and urethane primers instead of lacquer primer-surfacer, you will have to wait two weeks or more for each coat of that to dry before sanding and sealing. Remember, lacquer continues to shrink for a long time. If you sand too soon, sand scratches and other defects will show up later. You can count on that.

Color sanding of lacquer should be done with a good quality 600 wet or dry paper with a solid block. I have found that Norton paper works very well and tends to hold up better than 3M. You may also want to try the new Meguiar's waterproof paper. It is supposed to have more even grit than either Norton or 3M. Do not use a block that is too soft as it will not level the finish properly. The finish is sanded sufficiently when there are no more shiny spots on the surface. The idea is to get rid of all orange peel. This finish should then be

circle sanded by hand with a 1/4 sheet of Norton or Meguiar's 1200 paper and water.

The next step is to polish the surface with a power buffer. After much experimenting and after some advice from an expert restorer, I have found that the type of machine you use and the pad makes all the difference in buffing. The machine should operate at 1750 rpm. I recommend a Milwaukee model 5455. The best pad for initial buffing is the 3M 05705 yellow pad which is a two sided pad with a 5/8 inch threaded hole designed for professional machines. This pad requires an adapter to extend the length of the shaft. Keep the pad clean by periodically using a cleaning tool called a spur against the wheel while it is turning. A light compound such as Crest Light, available from Crest Industries, is good for a properly sanded finish. Buff until there are no more scratches showing from the 600 paper. I have found that other types of compound clog the pad and cause more scratches.

Some tips for buffing include: Hold the buffer at a slight angle to the surface with the wheel turning away from the edges. Buff large flat areas first and then work carefully on the peaks and high spots to prevent burning through. Hold the buffer in a comfortable position and be careful that the cord does not get in the wheel. Make sure that the rotation of the buffer is toward the ground so that you can pull up on it and prevent burn through. One trick is to put masking tape on the sharp edges and high spots as you are buffing the large panels to prevent them from burning through too quickly. Use soap and water and a sponge after compounding to remove all residue. Dry with a paper towel. If you can still see sanding marks, you have not buffed it enough.

Finish off the polishing with 3M Imperial Glaze #05991 using a machine with Meguiars sponge pad. You can also finish off with Meguiars #3 and wipe off with a diaper. By this time, if you did everything correctly, you should see a finish that will make you wonder if you really did it yourself. It will look like glass.

Painting the body (Acrylic Urethane)
A relatively new method of finishing is the use of acrylic urethane materials such as PPG Deltron

or duPont ChromaOne. Do not confuse this Deltron with the Deltron Basecoat/Clearcoat system which for some reason uses the same name on the can label. Acrylic urethane finishes are probably the most modern high technology finishes available today and provide a great many advantages over lacquer or enamel. Finishes like Deltron offer the fast film build and excellent dried gloss characteristics of enamel with the ease of application and fast drying speed of acrylic lacquer. In addition, they offer exceptional durability of color and gloss.

We will assume as before that you have started with a good base of DP 40 or equivalent primer and primer surfacer properly sanded and sealed as a preparation for the final finish. The finish should always be gone over with a good wax and grease remover such as PPG DX 330 or duPont Prep Sol 3919 if there is silicone present. You can never be too clean if you expect the finish to adhere. Remember, from the metal prep process forward, do not use anything but a paper towel on the surface. Any cloth or shop towels may be contaminated.

We will discuss the application of Deltron here but remember to always follow the directions on the label. Application of duPont or any other acrylic urethane finish will be similar.

Mix the Deltron according to the directions on the can. The standard mix calls for equal parts of Deltron color, Deltron DAU 2 catalyst and Deltron reducer such as DTU 504 for average shop conditions. The Deltron should be sprayed at 40-50 pounds pressure at the gun. Apply two or three wet coats if you are not going to rub out the finish, three to four if you are going to sand and compound. You will find the best results if you allow about 20 minutes flash time between coats. The best system is to apply one wet coat, wait 1-3 hours and then sand with 1200 Norton or Meguiar's paper. Apply two or three more coats and wait a full thirty days for the Deltron to fully cure. If you are not going to rub out the finish, you may want to try adding equal parts Delglo DAU 82 Clear catalyzed and thinned to reduced color for the final coat.

Even though Deltron dries faster than enamel, you should not handle it for at least a couple of hours. Be sure to get the literature on the proper and safe use of Deltron from your PPG dealer. It is very important that you use proper breathing equipment with any acrylic urethane materials as they contain isocyanates which are very toxic. If used indoors, you should have self contained breathing equipment. Outdoors, you need at least a very good respirator. Do not take these warnings lightly, as this stuff is deadly and is not to be used carelessly.

The reason I mentioned not rubbing out the Deltron finish is that it has an excellent gloss from just the normal application. If you are not building a national show winner, you may find that the finish as it is applied looks great. Although PPG does not recommend rubbing out the Deltron finish, with proper color sanding and compounding it can look as good or even better than any lacquer or hardened enamel job.

The sanding an finishing are very much the same as with the lacquer finish except that it is very important to wait at least 30 days before trying to work the finish. It takes Deltron 30 days to totally harden and you will find that until it is fully cured it can be damaged easily and will not finish properly.

The next step is to block sand with 1200 paper. Be sure to use a large block with not too soft a texture. Most of the commercial blocks and rubber pads are too soft and will follow the uneven contours too easily. A 1/4 inch piece of clear soft acrylic material works well if you can find it. When all of the orange peel is removed and the surface is dull and smooth, finish with an unfolded 1/4 sheet of 1200 paper. Finish the polishing using the same methods described in the lacquer section. You will find that you have completed a paint job that you can be proud of.

Many restorers do not like to do body work and painting, but it is a good feeling to know that all of the praise for that beautiful paint job will be for you. The finishing touch on that new restoration is the thing that enhances all of the other work, and the pride in knowing that you have done it yourself is worth all of the work and sweat.

Installing the wood in an 82B cab

Most trucks will be found in a condition that reflects the years of use and abuse they have suffered. The body wood will usually need to be replaced to give the proper strength and support to your truck. It is also necessary on the Ford body to have a solid wood framework for trim installation. Correct wood kits are available for almost all body types and although we will only cover the 82B here, many of the requirements will be the same for the other types.

The first step is to check the rough fit of all wood components to the body frame and to each other. The first piece to install is the windshield header, or front roof rail A-57238 as it is called in the body parts list. It should fit easily into the upper front of the body and fit flush against the mounting metal at each corner and across the bottom. The header is attached with two 5/16 inch flat head machine screws, washers, lockwashers and square nuts on each side. The nuts and washers should be at the front of the assembly. The heads of the screws should fit into the countersunk holes on the inside of the metal header. The bottom of the wood header will be further secured by the final attachment of the windshield frame when it is installed later.

The next piece to install is the rear roof rail A-83936. It is attached first at each corner with a 1/4 inch carriage bolt that goes through the brackets on each side of the back. The ends of the rear roof rail will butt to the lock pillars. The lower carriage bolts will be installed when the side roof rails and their brackets are installed.

Next install the roof side rails to the front and rear brackets A-83944 with appropriate carriage bolts, washers, lockwashers and nuts. The side rail mounting bracket carriage bolts will go through the lock pillar and the rear roof rail.

The next parts will be the roof side metal panels. These will be slipped around the bottom of the roof side rail. On the top, the roof rib support rails will be installed on the panels and secured to the rear roof rail with wood screws of proper length. The rails will be secured to the metal panels with eight #12 carriage bolts, nuts washers and lockwashers as shown in the photographs. The metal panels will then be nailed to the underside and outside of the side rails. Attach the front of the support rail to the front header gussets with carriage bolts, nuts, washers and lockwashers. The front corners of the panels should be nailed to the top of the wood header through the holes provided.

Next attach the three roof ribs A-47232 to the side support rails with #12 carriage bolts, nuts, washers and lockwashers, the nuts facing up as shown in the illustrations.

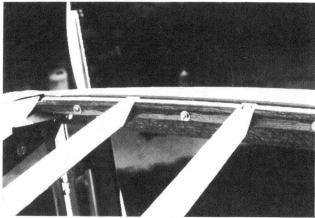

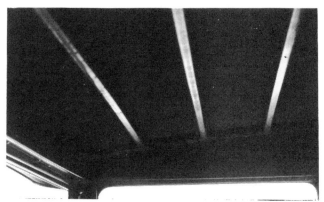

60

Spray gun tips

The air spray gun is to the automotive painter what the paint brush is to the artist. It is a precision tool used to apply the paint to the surface. The modern atomizer spray gun uses compressed air to atomize the sprayable material so that it may be applied to the car in the proper amounts and consistency. The spray gun, by means of air pressure, turns the liquid paint into tiny drops and by suction or pressure, forces the liquid out of the nozzle.

If you do much refinishing, it is important to have a good quality spray gun if you expect to achieve a quality finish. Binks and DeVilbiss are two brands of quality paint gun equipment which will give you good service and a quality finish. There are cheaper guns you can buy which are copies of these expensive guns. Outwardly, they look almost identical. If you are not going to do a lot of painting or maybe only one car, you might get by with one of these cheaper imported guns, but if you expect to do a few restorations, the quality tools are worth the price. If you saw a

demonstration of a comparison of the spray pattern and flow of the cheap guns and a good one, you would see a significant difference.

The eight main parts of a spray gun are: 1. The air cap; 2. The fluid cup; 3. The fluid needle valve; 4. The trigger; 5. The fluid control valve; 6. The air valve; 7. The pattern adjustment control valve, and 8. The cup assembly.

The cap directs the compressed air into the paint stream and atomizes it into a spray pattern, mixing air and paint outside the gun. The air flowing through the two horns of the cap form the shape of the spray pattern.

The pattern control valve controls the pattern by closing to make it rounder and opening to make the pattern longer in shape.

The fluid nozzle regulates the paint flowing through the fluid needle. The fluid control valve changes the position of the needle in its seat when the trigger is pulled.

The air valve is also operated by the trigger and is regulated by a screw adjustment on the back of the gun.

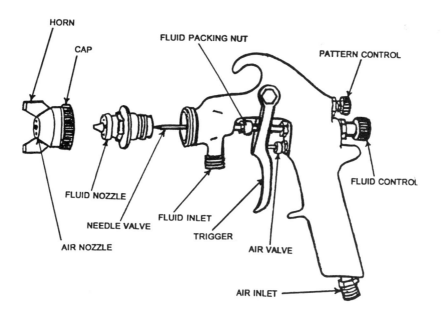

61

An air spray gun is operated by pulling back on the trigger which opens the air valve. In this first position, the trigger does not actuate the fluid needle and it functions as a blow gun. As the trigger is pulled further, it unseats the fluid needle and the gun begins to spray. The volume of paint leaving the tip of the gun is controlled by the pressure on the cup, the thickness of the paint, the size of the fluid orifice and by the fluid needle adjustment. Beyond these basic functions, the quality of the application is determined by the combination of the adjustments and trigger control that create the spray pattern.

A good spray pattern depends on the proper mixture of air and paint in the same manner that the running of a finely tuned engine depends on the proper mixture of fuel and air in the carburetor. The sprayed paint should go on smoothly in a medium to wet coat without sagging, running or orange peel.

Adjusting the spray gun should be accomplished in the correct order if you expect to achieve a fine finish. The first adjustment is the size of the spray pattern. This is adjusted using the pattern control valve to produce the desired fan according to the job at hand. The more the valve is opened, the wider the pattern.

The second adjustment is the fluid control valve which regulates the amount of paint according to the selected pattern width. Always set the fan size according to the size of the job and set the fluid to fill the fan.

The third adjustment is the air pressure, which is set at the regulator of the compressor. Remember that the pressure at the gun will not be the same as the pressure at the regulator. The difference will vary depending upon the length and diameter of the air hose. For this reason, pressure should be measured at the gun. For an example, a pressure reading at the compressor of 50 pounds if put through a 20 foot hose of 5/16 inch diameter will red only 46 pounds at the gun. If that hose was 1/4 inch, the same pressure would be 36 pounds. Look at the instructions on the paint container to see what pressures are required for the finish you are using.

Now that you have everything properly adjusted, try a test spray pattern on a piece of paper or cardboard. Hold the gun six to eight inches from the panel for lacquer and eight to ten inches away for enamel. Pull the trigger all the way and release. If the pattern is too coarse or too wet, increase the air pressure five pounds. If the pattern is too fine or too dry, open the fluid control valve slightly or decrease the pressure five pounds. The length of the pattern should be about nine inches from top to bottom. Make a couple of test passes on the panel and look at the pattern again. If the paint particles are too small or dry, open the fluid control valve slightly. If the paint is too wet or sagging, close the fluid valve.

To create a proper spray pattern on the job, always hold the gun the proper distance from the panel and keep it level and perpendicular to the surface. Do not move the gun in an arc or tilt it. Move the gun in a steady deliberate pass of about one foot per second and release at the end of each pass. This will avoid building up too much paint at the end of the panel and it will decrease overspray. Always begin at the top of a panel with the first pass. The second pass should come back the opposite direction overlapping the first by one half. This is considered a single coat. For a double coat, repeat the process immediately. See the books and pamphlets available from duPont, PPG and Binks for additional tips on using spray paint equipment. Always follow the manufacturer's recommendations on using all finish products. Most importantly, always observe all safety precautions as most materials are toxic and dangerous if used incorrectly. Always wear an approved respirator and in case of indoor use of catalyzed material, use an approved self-contained air system.

Many of the products and equipment for spraying will be changing in the future due to pollution considerations. Keep up with these changes by constantly reviewing the manufacturer's new product literature and seminars.

It is not very often that a government mandated pollution control law brings about the development of a product that makes our restoration project better, but HVLP is just that. The development of High Volume Low Pressure paint systems were mandated originally by air pollution requirements in Southern California. These laws require that paint spraying for automobiles must be accomplished with an efficiency of 65% or more. As with most pollution laws, what happens in California will soon happen to the rest of the country. The purpose is to reduce the amount of overspray which becomes airborne and contributes to emission of what are called Volatile Organic Compounds.

The answer to this overspray problem came with these new systems which transfer the materials to your car with no more than 10 p.s.i. This significant reduction in spraying pressure reduces overspray and thus emissions considerably. Some of the new HVLP systems transfer 65% to as much as 85% of the material to the surface. In addition to a reduction of overspray by about one-half, this increased efficiency also reduces your costs by allowing you to put more paint on the car and less as waste into the atmosphere. You will also gain from less contamination of filter systems and reduced exposure to toxic materials for yourself.

There are different methods of approach to the HVLP system by different manufacturers, but the end result is similar. Both Binks and DeVilbiss have guns which are developed from their existing guns and are designed to be used with a conventional compressor. They look similar to conventional paint guns other than the large fan control holes visible in the cap.

The other approach is the turbine systems like the ones offered by Croix, TiP and AccuSpray. These units are designed for and must be used with a special turbine which sounds much like a vacuum cleaner when running. The air is directed to the gun by means of a one inch diameter hose. One of the additional benefits of the turbine systems is that the air is heated as it is transferred to the paint gun. This heated air heats the paint as it is applied and tends to make the material flow better. You might find a reduction in runs and sags due to the fact that the heated material will flash off quicker than it would at a cooler temperature.

If you already have a good air compressor then the advantages of the turbine systems may be outweighed by the cost. A good turbine HVLP system costs about the same as a conventional compressor and paint gun. If you already have the compressor, you should consider one of the guns which give the benefits of HVLP while utilizing your existing compressor. The cost of these is similar to that of a good conventional gun.

You will have to make some changes in your painting practices with HVLP systems. One is that you will have to learn adjust the gun to your particular needs. In most cases, this will not be difficult as the adjustments are much the same as with a conventional spray system.

The main difference in operation with most HVLP systems is that you will be using considerably closer spraying distances than you might be used to with conventional spray guns. Six inches will not be unusual in most cases. Most HVLP guns will require different nozzles to handle the various types of materials and maintain proper spray distances and consistency.

The advent of HVLP is definitely an improvement in painting operations in every way. The reduction of overspray and what that will do to the quality of your finish is significant and that along with a savings in materials and work make the HVLP something you should take the time to study. Read all the literature and go to any available seminars of the manufacturers to decide which HVLP system is right for you. Check with your local dealer or see the ads in Hemmings and other old car publications for manufacturers of HVLP equipment.

TOP MOLDINGS AND DRIP RAIL

1/2 inch aluminum front molding used on 82B body.

Steel drip moldings used on fabric roof 82B body. This drip molding has a top material insert folded into the center to cover the nails.

9/16 inch steel used on rear of 82B body.

Cotton batting installed over the chicken wire on an 82A closed cab body.

1/2 inch steel used on front of 82B body

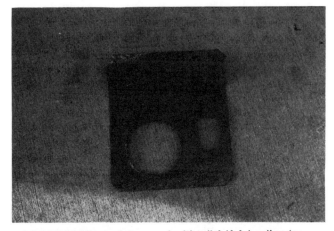

AA-82245 Floor plate used with all A/AA bodies to allow tower clearance when equipped with four-speed transmission. This should be painted with black enamel. I do not know of any reproductions available of this part.

AA Service Letter Notes

March 10, 1931

It has been decided to use AA-82766 door assembly, less paint and trim as standard equipment on Model 199A, Large Ice body in addition to Model 229B Service body on which it has already been specified as standard equipment. The AA-82766 door assembly has a depression in it and is to be used with a closed cab when the spare wheel is carried in a fender well. This door assembly is also available as special equipment for Model 242A and all dump truck bodies when tires larger than 6.00-20 are used.

A change is being made in the AA Panel and A Panel drop floor trim changing from the present blue-gray to a cobra cross grain. This change has already been put into effect and on any parts which you requisition for replacement on cars, do not fail to specify the color desired.

May 26, 1931

A new design running board is released for 131 1/2" wheelbase truck with dual rear wheels and rear fender to be used with dual wheels on models 195A, 280A, 285A, 300A and 197A. Dual wheel rear fenders for AA Panel 131 1/2" 85B, Regular Patrol 290A, Service Car 229A will be released at a later date. The parts affected by this change are as follows:
AA-16312 Rear fender assembly (Dual) RH
AA-16313 Rear fender assembly (Dual) LH
AA-16337 Spacer rear fender to wheel house panel 195A & 197A
AA-16508 Running board assembly RH
AA-16509 Running board assembly LH
The running board assemblies are specified to be used on all 131 1/2" wheelbase trucks with dual rear wheel rear fenders
AA-16500 Running board assembly RH
AA-16501 Running board assembly LH
(Used on 210A and now specified for 197A through service)

September 1, 1931

Linoleum covered running boards have been released for use on the ambulance 280A and Funeral coach 275A bodies for improved appearance, replacing the metal running board used at the present. This change is effective as soon as stock is received and any built-up jobs on hand should have this equipment installed also. The parts affected by this change are as follows:
AA-16475 Running board assembly RH
AA-16476 Running board assembly LH
New number and new design specified for use open Models 275A and 280A replacing AA-16458-B and AA-16459-B.

Front end assembly for A and AA commercial chassis, less body which is also used on the school bus, has been changed so that the rear face of the front end frame is perpendicular, permitting a better fit for bodies built for use with this front end. This affects the front end frame assembly, cowl side panels, floor side sill front and front end frame finish panel.

A tail gate assembly has been released for Model 185B Platform 157" and 187A Platform 131 1/2" and will be supplied as special equipment at extra cost for those desiring it as outlined in recent Sales Department letter. This tail gate is attached to the floor by four hinges, also a chain 151" long is supplied with the tail gate. A new tail gate assembly, including chain has symbol AA-185600 and is available through production or service as special equipment at extra cost for those that wish a tail gate that drops down and is hinged to the floor. The 151" chain permits lowering the gate to the level of the floor for unloading purposes.

September 3, 1931

A tail gate for 131 1/2" and 157" stake bodies is now available. The height of this tail gate from the top of the platform is 19". It is equipped with three strong hinges and 151" of chain to enable the gate to be opened to any desired position.

Combination grain and stock bodies are now available. These bodies are 84 " wide, are of hard wood construction throughout with exceptionally heavy flooring and the side and flare boards are rigidly supported by malleable iron brackets.

Extension grain sides are provided, making the body 26" deep. There is a hinged door in the tail gate. The sliding tail gate may be completely removed or fixed at any desired height. Stock racks fit into the same pocket as the extension grain sides. The stock rack tail gate is painted white for good visibility at night. These bodies are available with either 131" or 157" chassis.

December 9, 1931

Dual wheel rear fenders are released for use on the Model 315A Standrive Delivery body as special equipment for sale through service or for assembly on our assembly line. The fenders used are the same as those used on Models 210A and AA Panel.

AA-16310 Rear fender assembly RH
AA-16311 Rear fender assembly LH
AA-16348 Rear fender to body anti-squeak 2 required
A-20718S2 Bolt, rear fender to body 4 required
A-20721S2 Bolt, " " " 10 required
A-21707S2 Nut, " " " 2 required
A-22217S2 Washer, " " " 14 required
       " Body to rear fender 2 required
A-22219S2 Washer, rear fender to body 14 required

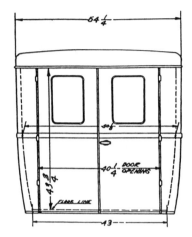

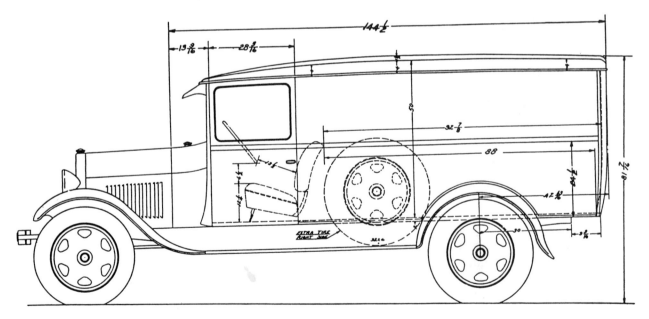

MODEL AA TRUCK WITH PANEL BODY

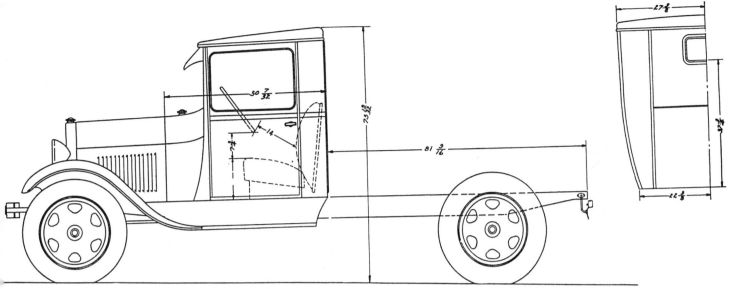

MODEL AA CHASSIS WITH CLOSED CAB

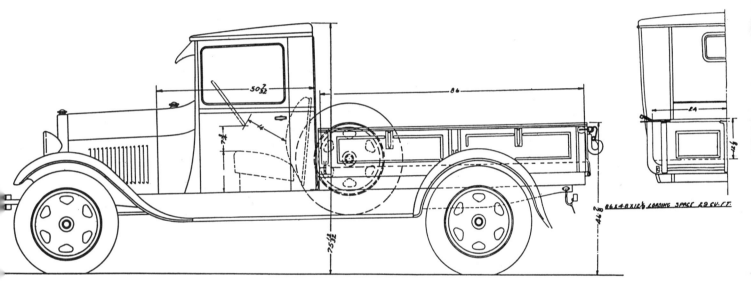

MODEL AA TRUCK, CLOSED CAB AND EXPRESS BODY

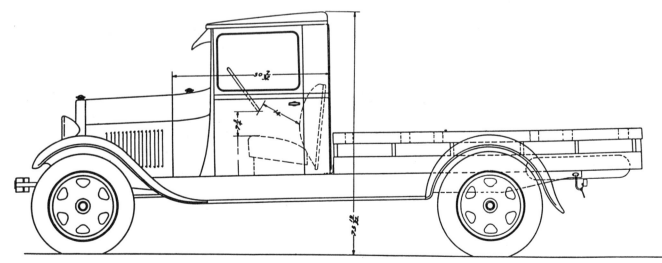

MODEL AA TRUCK, CLOSED CAB AND PLATFORM BODY

67

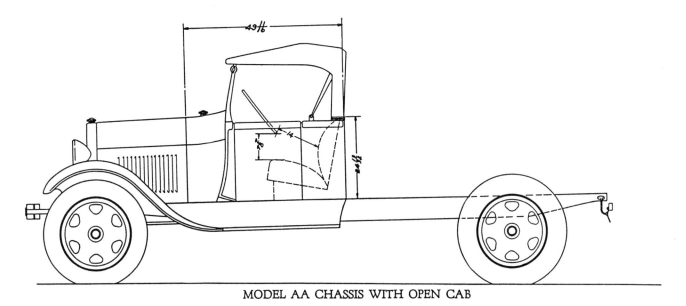

MODEL AA CHASSIS WITH OPEN CAB

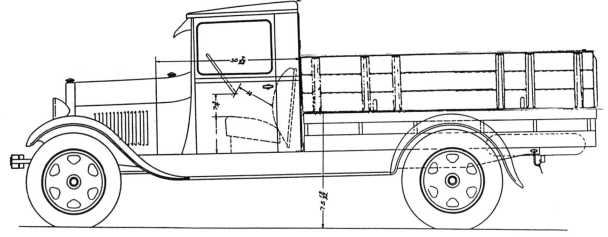

AA TRUCK WITH CLOSED CAB AND GRAIN BODY

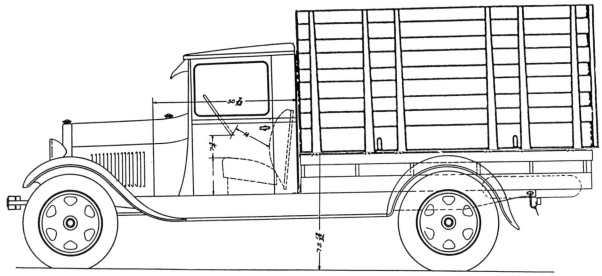

MODEL AA TRUCK, CLOSED CAB AND STAKE BODY

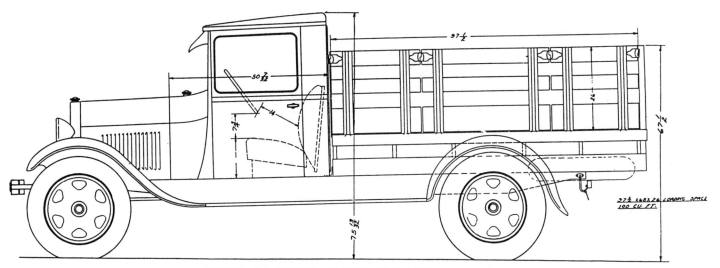

MODEL AA TRUCK, CLOSED CAB AND STAKE BODY

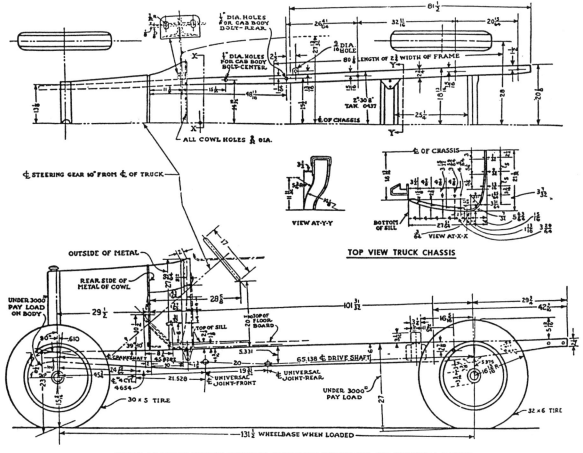

TOP VIEW TRUCK CHASSIS

MODEL AA TRUCK CHASSIS SHOWING IMPORTANT DIMENSIONS FOR MOUNTING BODIES

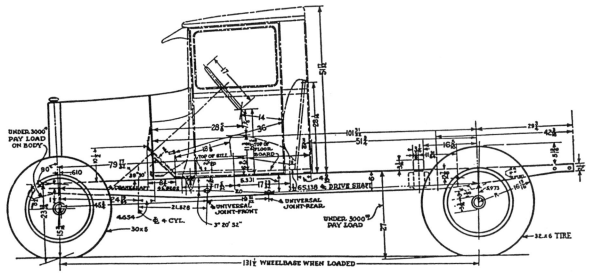

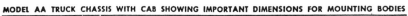

MODEL AA TRUCK CHASSIS WITH CAB SHOWING IMPORTANT DIMENSIONS FOR MOUNTING BODIES

AA 131 TRUCK WITH 85B PANEL DELIVERY BODY

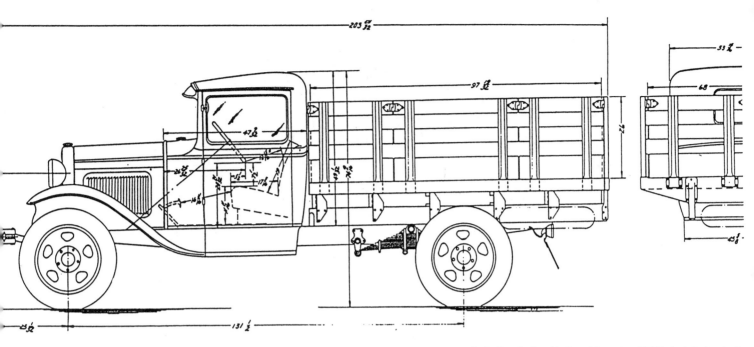

CLOSED CAB 82-B WITH PLATFORM 88-A AND
STAKE RACKS 188-A ON AA-CHASSIS

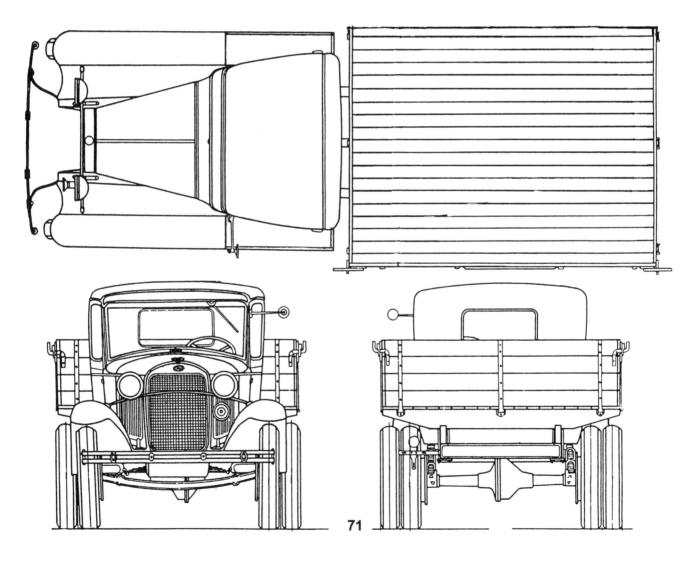

71

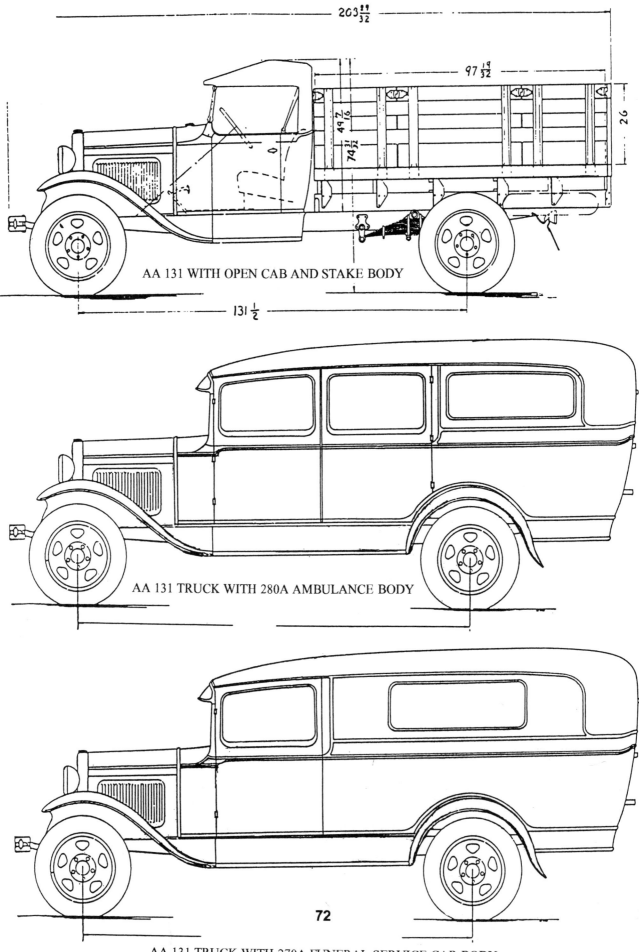

$203\frac{11}{32}$

$97\frac{19}{32}$

26

$49\frac{7}{16}$

$74\frac{31}{32}$

AA 131 WITH OPEN CAB AND STAKE BODY

$131\frac{1}{2}$

AA 131 TRUCK WITH 280A AMBULANCE BODY

72

AA 131 TRUCK WITH 270A FUNERAL SERVICE CAR BODY

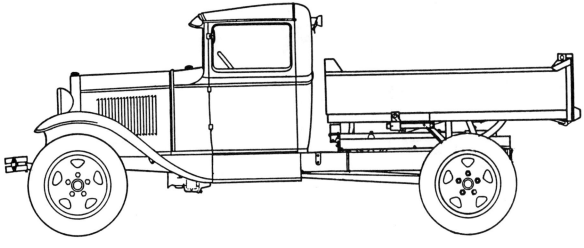

AA 131 WITH ROTATING FAST HAND HOIST DUMP BODY

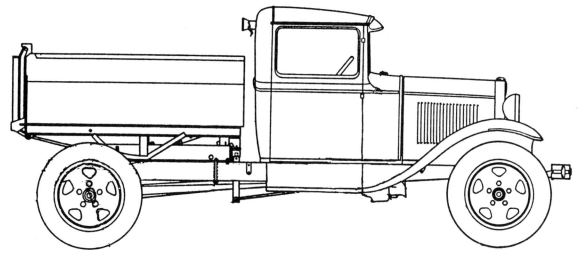

AA 131 WITH GRAVITY DUMP BODY

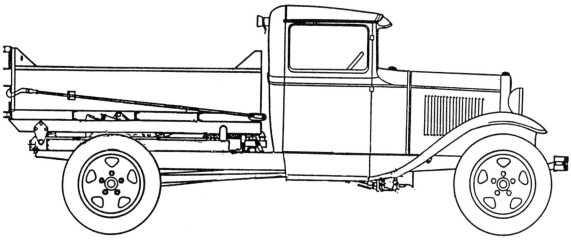

AA 131 WITH HEAVY DUTY HYDRAULIC DUMP BODY

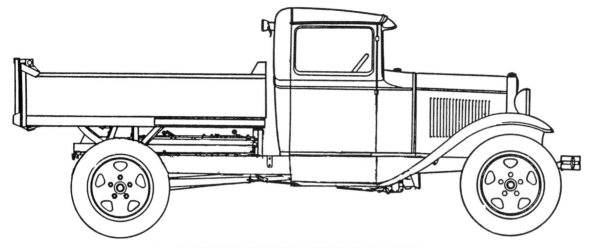

AA 131 WITH ROTATING POWER HOIST DUMP BODY

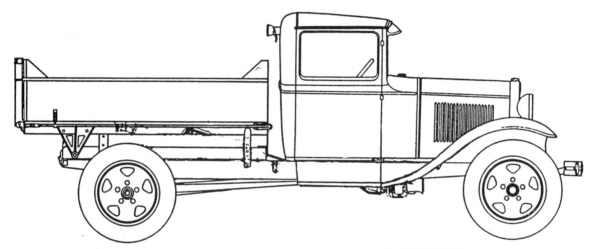

AA 131 WITH LIGHT DUTY HYDRAULIC DUMP BODY

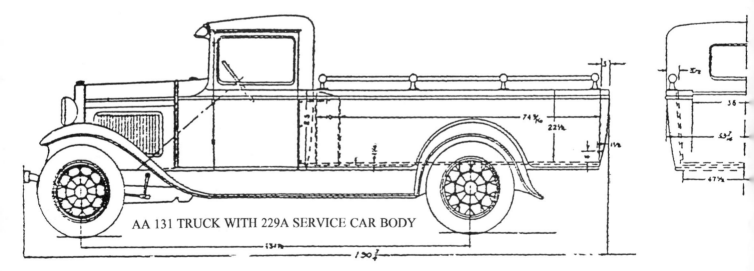

AA 131 TRUCK WITH 229A SERVICE CAR BODY

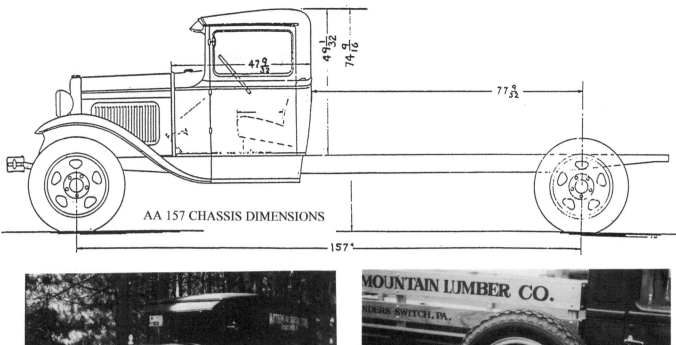

AA 157 CHASSIS DIMENSIONS

$49\frac{1}{32}$

$74\frac{9}{16}$

$47\frac{9}{32}$

$77\frac{9}{32}$

157"

75

Early 1930 AA truck with 1929 style body.

A September, 1929 AA-131 Fire truck with General body and equipment using the AA commercial cowl. This truck has a low-speed worm drive rear axle and four-speed transmission.

An excellent example of an early 1930 truck with a 1929 body. Notice the bumper, steering wheel, gas cap, headlights and wheels, which are all early 1930 parts. It is believed that the cowl tank may have used an adapter to accommodate the 1930-31 style filler cap.

A late 1930 truck with a long running board and shield assembly and commercial cowl. Notice the upper band across the cowl which replaces the windshield frame.

This truck was used as a fire truck and has the rare AA-17757-A chrome bumper bars.

An excellent late 1930 AA-131 with dump body.

An example of a non-Ford commercial delivery body mounted on a 1930 AA-131 chassis.

A 1931 AA truck with grain body and cover.

SUPPLEMENT TO
Chapter 13

SPECIAL EQUIPMENT

THIS chapter will deal with the final portion of the Ford Parts number system, which is called special equipment. This group includes shock absorbers, mirrors, bumpers etc. In the Parts Price List, the number group of AA-17000 and over also includes accessories and tools. In this shop manual, we will also discuss whatever other miscellaneous items which do not appear elsewhere or may not be extensive enough to warrant a full chapter.

Rear View Mirror Service Letter Notes

March 10, 1931

The method of fastening the rear view mirror to brackets for commercial jobs has been changed from the use of a set screw in the end of the bracket to an acorn nut on the end of the mirror swivel plug, which is now threaded. Also, the bracket has been changed in shape and has one hole for fastening the bracket to the door hinge instead of two. The bracket for the Deluxe delivery, 130B, as you will note from the instructions below is changed from black to chrome plate. We list below the various parts affected by this change:

A-17723-A, Rear view mirror assembly, chrome plate, has been specified as standard equipment to be used on the Deluxe delivery, Model 130B, Station wagon, 150B and Special delivery, 255A replacing A-1772-R for production.

A-17723-B, Rear view mirror assembly. black enamel, has been specified to be used as standard equipment on the A Panel 79B, A Panel drop floor, 225A, Closed cab, 82B and AA Panel, 85B, replacing A-17738-R for production.

A-17724-A, Rear view mirror supporting arm to swivel acorn nut, chrome plated, is specified to be used in conjunction with A-17723-A listed above.

A-17724-B, Rear view mirror support arm to swivel acorn nut, black enamel, specified to be used as standard equipment and for service on the following bodies: A Panel, 79B, A Panel drop floor, 225A, Station wagon, 150B, Special delivery 255A, Closed cab, 82B and AA Panel, 85B.

A-17741-C, Rear view mirror bracket, black enamel, specified to be used as standard equipment on the Station wagon, 150B and Special delivery, 255A. This is a new number and new part, replacing A-17741-AR in production.

A-17742-A, Rear view mirror bracket, chrome plated, specified to be used on Deluxe delivery 130B, replacing A-17741-B in production.

A-17742-B, Rear view mirror bracket, black enamel, specified to be used as standard equipment on A Panel, 79B, A Panel drop floor, 225A, AA Panel, 85B, and Closed cab, 82B, except when used with Platform, 187A and 185B, Express, 195A, 197A and 242A, Dump, Coal or Garbage bodies, Police patrol, 290A.

AA-17745-C, Rear view mirror bracket, specified to be used with closed cabs when used with 195A, 197A and 242A, Express bodies 187A and 185B, Platform bodies, Dump, Coal or Garbage bodies. This part is the same as the AA-17745-BR except that the outer end is redesigned eliminating the set screw hole.

September 1, 1931

To improve rear vision, the rear view mirror bracket for the Model 210A, AA Panel delivery unit has been increased 1-1/8" in length. Parts affected by this change are as follows:

AA-17697-B, Rear view mirror bracket 10" long. This is a new number and new length specified to be used on each Model 210A Panel delivery body assembled.

To improve rear vision, a larger rear view mirror part AA-17704 is released for use on the school bus. The new design is 3-1/2" wide and 9-1/2" long and replaces A-17704 for use on the school bus only and will be used starting at once.

A-17741-A Rear view mirror and bracket assembly on 82A closed cab body.

A-17741-B Rear view mirror and bracket on 82B closed cab body. This basic design bracket was used in various lengths up to the AA-17745-C which is 10 7/8 in. long. In May, 1931 a new AA-17698 bracket was released for platform and coal bodies which is 11 11/16 in. long.

AA Bumpers

The early 1928 to early 1930 AA trucks were equipped with the same bumper assembly as the Model A car but listed it as AA-17750-A in the Parts Price List. When the truck body style was changed in June, 1930, Ford changed to the Seldom seen chrome plated bumper which used AA-17757-A bars. These resemble the 1930-31 car bumpers, but are wider and thicker. This assembly was not used on all trucks. It was seen later on some deluxe AA Models and was offered as an option for a while. This bumper assembly is illustrated in this chapter.

In November, 1930, the new single bar AA-17750-B, Front bumper assembly, which used the black enamel AA-17757-B bar. This bumper utilized a new design AA-17760-B back bar. The entire single bar front bumper assembly was carried over to the 1932 BB trucks with a change only in the Numbers. A BB front bumper assembly will fit a AA truck. This bumper assembly is illustrated in this chapter.

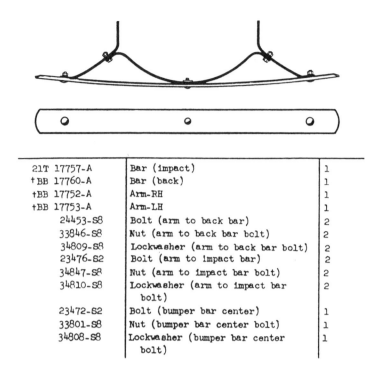

21T 17757-A	Bar (impact)	1
†BB 17760-A	Bar (back)	1
†BB 17752-A	Arm-RH	1
†BB 17753-A	Arm-LH	1
24453-S8	Bolt (arm to back bar)	2
33846-S8	Nut (arm to back bar bolt)	2
34809-S8	Lockwasher (arm to back bar bolt)	2
23476-S2	Bolt (arm to impact bar)	2
34847-S8	Nut (arm to impact bar bolt)	2
34810-S8	Lockwasher (arm to impact bar bolt)	2
23472-S2	Bolt (bumper bar center)	1
33801-S8	Nut (bumper bar center bolt)	1
34808-S8	Lockwasher (bumper bar center bolt)	1

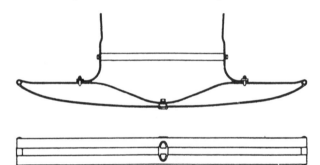

†AA 17757-A	Bar (bumper front)	2
† AA 17760-A	Bar (bumper back)	1
†AA 17756	Plate (bumper bar clamp back)	1
†A 17758-B	Clamp (bumper bar center)-front	1
33848-S7	Nut (bumper bar center clamp)	1
34810-S7	Lockwasher (center clamp)	1
†AA 17752-A	Arm-RH	1
†AA 17753-A	Arm-LH	1
†AA 17915	Bolt (arm to back bar)	2
33802-S8	Nut (arm to back bar bolt)	4
34808-S8	Lockwasher (arm to back bar bolt)	4
†AA 17916	Plate (arm to back bar bolt)	2
A 17766	Stud (arm to back frame)	2
A 17767	Stud (arm to back frame)	2
33846-S8	Nut (arm to frame stud)	4
34809-S8	Lockwasher (arm to frame stud)	4
†AA 17773	Bar (front bumper cross)	1
24453-S8	Bolt (front bumper cross bar)	2
34809-S8	Lockwasher (cross bar bolt)	2
†AA 17920	Bolt (bumper end)	2
33927-S7	Nut (bumper end bolt)	2
34808-S8	Lockwasher (bumper end bolt)	2

A close look at the rare AA-17757-A bumper bars mounted on a late 1930 AA chassis. They are noticeably wider and thicker than Model a car bumpers.

Bumper Service Letter Notes

May 26, 1931

A new rear bumper assembly has been released for production on various truck models and of course, is available for service. The complete rear bumper assembly bears the symbol AA-17814-B, while the rear bumper assembly right hand, is covered by AA-17815-B, and the left hand by AA-17816-B, these later two numbers cover the sub-assemblies of the complete bumper assembly.

September 1, 1931

A rear bumper for use on the Model 210A Panel delivery unit has been released for service and will be installed on our final assembly line on request from the dealers. This bumper assembly is of the cross bar type, using the regular standard truck front bumper assembly. The component parts which go to make up this assembly are as follows:

1-AA-17757, Bumper bar
1-AA-17975, Rear bumper back bar
1-AA-17921, Rear bumper arm right hand
1-AA-17922, Rear bumper arm left hand
1-A-21169S2 Bolt
1-A-21787S1 Nut
1-A-22300S1 Washer-lock rear bumper cross bar
           to back bar
2-A-21219S4 Bolt
2-A-21845S1 Nut
2-A-22330S1 Lock washer-rear bumper arm to
           back bar
2-A-21280S4 Bolt, rear bumper arm to cross bar
2-A-21880S1 Nut "   "   "   "
2-A-22355S1 Washer "   "   "   "
4-A-21219S4 Bolt, rear bumper arm to frame
4-A-21845S1 Nut "   "   "
2-A-22330S1 Washer "   "   "   "

Shock absorbers

Early 1928-29 AA trucks equipped with the standard Model A front axle were equipped with shock absorbers on the front only. The shock absorbers were the same as the car but were equipped with AA-18047 front shock absorber arms.

Late 1929-31 trucks equipped with the new, heavier front axle were not equipped with front shock absorbers. There is no provision for attachment of shock absorbers on the front spring perch.

In 1931, certain Models of AA truck were equipped with rear shock absorbers. These units looked similar to the Model A car units, but were given the parts numbers AA-18008, and AA-18009, Rear shock absorber and link.

AA Shock Absorber Service Letter Notes

April 3, 1931

AA shock absorbers are being listed as standard equipment for the rear of the Funeral Service Car, the Funeral Coach and the Ambulance, and of course, will be available for service or installation on any other jobs on which you may desire to install them.

Also, the long muffler tailpipes will be used on these jobs, together with the rear spring which is 12 inches longer. It is recommended that the shock absorbers be installed only on the jobs which are already equipped with the 12" longer springs. These springs should only be installed on those jobs where increased riding comfort is desired and where it is known that the truck will not be overloaded. The long muffler tailpipe will also be used on the above jobs.

The following are the parts and numbers which are affected by the installation of the shock absorbers, the new rear spring and the long muffler tailpipe:

A-21247 Bolt, rear shock absorber to frame
AA-5253 Muffler outlet pipe, long
AA-5256-D Muffler outlet pipe bracket to side
           member
AA-5558-D Rear spring assembly
AA-18015 Rear shock absorber assembly RH
AA-18016 Rear shock absorber assembly LH
AA-18056 Rear shock absorber link and ball
           assembly
AA-18092 Rear axle shock absorber support
           assembly RH
AA-18093 Rear axle shock absorber support
           assembly LH

Miscellaneous

AA Radiator Shell Service Letter Notes

March 10, 1931

The symbol numbers on the radiator shell assembly, black enamel, also on the radiator name plate assembly, have been changed from A to AA, in other words, change the listing in your Model A Parts List from A-8212-AR, Radiator name plate to AA-8212, A-8200-A Radiator shell assembly, black enamel, the "A" being added to the symbol number to distinguish it from the AA-8200-B rustless steel design.

July 8, 1931

To facilitate the identifying of the radiator name plate, we are giving below the symbol numbers and description of the parts in question:

A-8212-B Shipped with the name Ford and outer ring in prime coat

A-8212-C Shipped finished with Ford name and outer ring in black enamel

AA-8212 Shipped finished with Ford name chrome plate and blue enamel background (was formerly carried as A-8212-A)

AA-8005-B radiator looks similar to the Model A radiator at first glance, but it has four rows of tubes and is thicker. It requires the AA-8260 upper hose.

Electrical system

One difference in the AA electrical system is the 315A Standrive chassis, which has a higher output generator than the standard Model A. This was accomplished primarily with a different generator pulley assembly.

The other difference is the A-14578-D, Non-metallic conduit for the headlights and the A-14582-C non-metallic conduit for the horn. These are used on the AA chassis, 76B, 78A, 79B, 82B, 85B, 88A, 88B, 89A, 185B and 225A.

These conduits were introduced in a Service Letter dated August 18, 1930. They are made from a flexible loom with a glossy black finish as compared to the nickel and rustless steel conduits used on the earlier trucks and on the A chassis. A duplicate of these may be fabricated using the normal conduit ends and attaching or clamping a proper length fabric lacquered wire available from an automotive wiring supplier such as Rhode Island Wiring.

A close look at the AA-8200-A black enamel radiator shell. The AA-8200-B is identical in design, but is made of stainless steel. This March, 1931 truck has a name plate with a blue background as indicated in Service letter.

Exhaust system

The AA truck was equipped in its early versions with the same muffler and tailpipe assembly as the Model A Car, but by early 1931, special tailpipe equipment was being installed on various AA chassis. See page 558 of the April 1931 Service Bulletins and the appropriate edition of the Ford Parts Price List for details on lengths and design of muffler and tailpipe assemblies. New stainless steel muffler/tailpipe assemblies are now available which closer replicate the original design and sound of the Model A. The manufacturer of one of these has assured me that he will fabricate a special AA muffler and tailpipe assembly to your specifications if requested.

Governor unit

Some A and AA trucks were originally equipped with governor units similar to the one pictured. These were installed by fleet owners to prevent serious engine damage by careless drivers. The design and construction of these units varied by manufacturer, so it is not possible to discuss them here. The one shown attached to the front timing cover and was operated electrically.

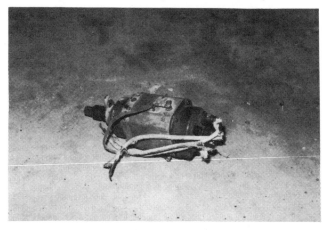

Fire equipment

Fire equipment was installed on the Model A and AA chassis by many different manufacturers. These fire trucks today add a great deal of interest to the A and AA chassis and ownership of this type of vehicle is enjoyed by many enthusiasts. The problems of restoration of the basic truck are made more difficult by the additional problems of restoring the pumps, racks, bodies and other special equipment that will be found on fire equipment. It may be advisable to join a group devoted to the preservation of this equipment so that you may find someone more familiar with the restoration of these items. Some fire equipment is pictured here from a late 1929 AA fire truck built by the General Fire Truck Company of St. Louis, Missouri.

85

SUPPLY AND SERVICE SOURCES

Clubs and organizations

American Truck Historical Society
300 Office Park Drive
Birmingham, AL 35253
205-870-0566

The Model A Ford Club of America
250 South Cypress Street
La Habra, CA 90631-5586
310-697-2712

Model A Restorer's Club
24800 Michigan Avenue
Dearborn, MI 48124-1713
313-278-1455

Parts suppliers

A&L Parts Specialties
Indian Hill Acres
Canton, Ohio 06019

Bratton's Antique Auto Parts
9410 Watkins Road
Gaithersburg, MD 20882
1-800-255-1929

Mark Auto Company, Inc.
Layton, NJ 07851
201-948-4157

Battlefield Antique
5054 South Broadview
Battlefield, MO 65619
417-882-7923

Mack Products
100 Fulton Avenue
Moberly, MO 65270
816-263-7444
Pickup truck book and parts

Smith and Jones Antique Ford
1 Biloxi Square
Columbia Airport
West Columbia, SC 29170
803-822-8502

Obsolete Ford Parts, Inc.
6601 South Shields
Oklahoma City, OK 73149
405-631-3933

Gaslight Auto Parts
P.O. Box 291
Urbana, Ohio 43078
513-652-2145
New sheet metal

LeBaron Bonney Company
P.O. Box 6, Chestnut St.
Amesbury, MA 01913
508-388-3811
Upholstery and tops

Antique Automotive
2451 State Street
San Diego, CA 92101
800-995-6626

Snyder's Antique Auto Parts
12925 Woodworth Road
New Springfield, OH 44443
216-549-5313

Pioneer Valley Model A Ford Inc.
81 East Street
Easthampton, MA 01027
413-584-8400

Mac's Antique Auto Parts
PO Box 312, 1051 Lincoln Ave.
Lockport, NY 14094
800-828-7948

Gene Renninger
2766 Old Phila. Pike
Bird-In-Hand, PA 17505

Sacramento Vintage Ford
4675 Aldoma Lane
Sacramento, CA 95841

Zanes Antique Cars & Pts
2008 Leland Way
Salina, KS 67401

Tin Lizzie Antique Auto
1549 Ellinwood
Des Plaines, IL 60016

Howell's Sheetmetal Co.
P.O. Box 179
Nome, TX 77629

Antique Auto Center
330 Bennett Road
Elk Grove Village, IL 60007
708-439-0010

C&J Early Ford Parts
117 Midland Ave.
Maryland Heights, MO 63043-1363
314-298-0487

Fritz Specialties, Inc.
Rt. 5 Berry Dairy Rd.
DeSoto, MO 63020
314-586-5336

Kano Laboratories
1000 South Thompson Lane
Nashville, TN 37211-2627
615-833-4101
Kroil Penetrating oil

The Eastwood Co.
580 Lancaster Ave.
Malvern, PA 19355-0714
800-345-1178

Coker Tire
1317 Chestnut Street
Chatanooga, TN 37402
800-251-6336
Tires

Lucas Automotive
2141 West Main
Springfield, OH 45504
513-324-1773
Tires

Ozark Early Ford Parts
1862 Yellow Rock Rd.
DeSoto, MO 63020

Birdhaven Vintage Auto
RR 1 Box 152
Colfax, IA 50054

Carlin MFG. Co.
PO Box 3591 1250 Gulf St
Beaumont, TX 77701

Early Ford Parts
2948 Sumner Ave.
Memphis, TN 38112

Beam's Antique Ford Parts
P.O. Box 568
Denver, NC 28037

Paul Ellis Ford Parts
312 Chapman Highway
Seymour, TN 37865

Donald Roberts Antique
RD #1 Mason Road
Mohawk, NY 13407

Beaver Mfg. Stainless Div.
Drawer 138
Marthasville, MO 63357
Stainless mufflers & pipes

Becker's T&A Ford Parts
595 S.W. 150th St.
Beaverton, OR 97006

AA BODY TYPES

MODEL AA FORD TRUCK—4 Cylinder Engine
(131½" and 157" Wheelbase)

P-970

1931

FORD COMMERCIAL AND TRUCK MODELS

BODY TYPE	NAME	BODY TYPE	NAME
65-A	Canopy and Screens (Used with Type 78-B)	204-B	Dump body with light hydraulic hoist (1½ cu. yd. capacity) (Wood)
66-A	De Luxe Pickup	205-A	Hi-Lift Hydraulic Coal Body (72 cu. ft.) (Wood)
76-B	Cab (Open)	206-B	Dump body with mechanical hoist (1½ cu. yd. capacity) (Detwiller)
78-A	Pickup		
78-B	Pickup	207-B	Combined dump and coal body with high sides and end gate with chute opening and swinging partition (1½ cu. yd. capacity) (120 cu. ft. with top boards)
79-A	Panel Delivery (103½" Wheelbase)		
79-B	Panel Delivery (103½" Wheelbase)		
82-B	Cab (Closed)		
85-B	Panel Delivery (131½" Wheelbase)	208-A	Dump body with heavy hydraulic hoist (1½ cu. yd. capacity) (Galion)
130-B	De Luxe Delivery (Drop Floor)		
130-B	De Luxe Delivery (Standard)	208-B	Dump body with heavy hydraulic hoist (1½ cu. yd. capacity) (Wood)
150-B	Station Wagon		
185-B	Platform (157" Wheelbase)	210-A	"AA" Panel Delivery
186-B	Stake (157" Wheelbase)	225-A	"A" Panel Delivery (with drop floor)
187-B	Platform (131½" Wheelbase)	228-A	Stock Racks
189-A	Stake (131½" Wheelbase)	229-A	Service Car
195-A	Express Body (131½" Wheelbase)	236-A	Light hydraulic hoist and body understructure (Galion)
196-A	Canopy Top and Screens (For 195-A)		
197-A	Express Body (157" Wheelbase)	236-B	Light hydraulic hoist and body understructure
198-A	Canopy Top and Screens (For 197-A)	237-A	Heavy hydraulic hoist and body understructure (Galion)
199-A	Ice Wagon		
200-B	Dump Body with hand hoist (1½ cu. yd. capacity) (Galion)	237-B	Heavy hydraulic hoist and body understructure (Wood)
201-A	Coal body with heavy hydraulic hoist and end gate with chute (less swinging partition) (75 cu. ft.) (Galion)	238-A	Stock Racks (157" Wheelbase)
		239-A	Meat Packers Express
		242-A	Heavy Duty Express Body (131½" Wheelbase)
201-B	Coal body with heavy duty hydraulic hoist, swinging partition and end gate with chute (high end) (75 cu. ft. or 120 cu. ft. with sides) (Wood)	244-A	Grain body with or without stock rack or grain side extensions) (157" Wheelbase)
		248-A	Grain body with or without stock rack or grain side extensions (131½" Wheelbase)
201-C	Coal body with heavy duty hydraulic hoist and end gate with chute (less swinging partition) (75 cu. ft.) (Wood)	255-A	Special Delivery (Natural Wood)
		270-A	Funeral Service
202-B	Gravity dump body (1½ cu. yd. capacity) (Wood)	275-A	Funeral Coach
203-A	Garbage body with heavy hydraulic hoist (2 cu. yd. capacity) (Galion)	280-A	Ambulance
		285-A	Police Patrol (De Luxe)
203-B	Garbage body with heavy hydraulic hoist (2 cu. yd. capacity) (Wood)	290-A	Police Patrol (Standard)
		295-A	Town Car Delivery
203-C	Garbage body with heavy hydraulic hoist (3 cu. yd. capacity) (Galion)	300-A	De Luxe Delivery
		315-A	Standrive
203-D	Garbage body with heavy hydraulic hoist (3 cu. yd. capacity) (Wood)	330-A	School and Passenger Bus
		400-A	Convertible Sedan
204-A	Dump body with light hydraulic hoist (1½ cu. yd. capacity) (Galion)		

GENERAL INFORMATION

DECIMAL EQUIVALENTS
OF WIRE, LETTER AND FRACTIONAL SIZE DRILLS

DRILL SIZE	DECIMAL	DRILL SIZE	DECIMAL	DRILL SIZE	DECIMAL
80	.0135	29	.1360	21/64	.3281
79	.0145	28	.1405	Q	.3320
1/64	.0156	9/64	.1406	R	.3390
78	.0160	27	.1440	11/32	.3438
77	.0180	26	.1470	S	.3480
76	.0200	25	.1495	T	.3580
75	.0210	24	.1520	23/64	.3594
74	.0225	23	.1540	U	.3680
73	.0240	5/32	.1562	3/8	.3750
72	.0250	22	.1570	V	.3770
71	.0260	21	.1590	W	.3860
70	.0280	20	.1610	25/64	.3906
69	.0292	19	.1660	X	.3970
68	.0310	18	.1695	Y	.4040
1/32	.0313	11/64	.1719	13/32	.4062
67	.0320	17	.1730	Z	.4130
66	.0330	16	.1770	27/64	.4219
65	.0350	15	.1800	7/16	.4375
64	.0360	14	.1820	29/64	.4531
63	.0370	13	.1850	15/32	.4688
62	.0380	3/16	.1875	31/64	.4844
61	.0390	12	.1890	1/2	.5000
60	.0400	11	.1910	33/64	.5156
59	.0410	10	.1935	17/32	.5313
58	.0420	9	.1960	35/64	.5469
57	.0430	8	.1990	9/16	.5625
56	.0465	7	.2010	37/64	.5781
3/64	.0469	13/64	.2031	19/32	.5938
55	.0520	6	.2040	39/64	.6094
54	.0550	5	.2055	5/8	.6250
53	.0595	4	.2090	41/64	.6406
1/16	.0625	3	.2130	21/32	.6562
52	.0635	7/32	.2188	43/64	.6719
51	.0670	2	.2210	11/16	.6875
50	.0700	1	.2280	45/64	.7031
49	.0730	A	.2340	23/32	.7188
48	.0760	15/64	.2344	47/64	.7344
5/64	.0781	B	.2380	3/4	.7500
47	.0785	C	.2420	49/64	.7656
46	.0810	D	.2460	25/32	.7812
45	.0820	E 1/4	.2500	51/64	.7969
44	.0860	F	.2570	13/16	.8125
43	.0890	G	.2610	53/64	.8281
42	.0935	17/64	.2656	27/32	.8438
3/32	.0938	H	.2660	55/64	.8594
41	.0960	I	.2720	7/8	.8750
40	.0980	J	.2770	57/64	.8906
39	.0995	K	.2810	29/32	.9062
38	.1015	9/32	.2812	59/64	.9219
37	.1040	L	.2900	15/16	.9375
36	.1065	M	.2950	61/64	.9531
7/64	.1094	19/64	.2969	31/32	.9688
35	.1100	N	.3020	63/64	.9844
34	.1110	5/16	.3125	1	1.000
33	.1130	O	.3160		
32	.1160	P	.3230		
31	.1200				
1/8	.1250				
30	.1285				

TAP DRILL SIZES
BASED ON APPROXIMATELY 75% FULL THREAD

THREAD	DRILL	THREAD	DRILL
#0—80	3/64	1-3/4—5	1-35/64
#1—64	No. 53	1-3/4—12	1-43/64
#1—72	No. 53	2-4-1/2	1-25/32
#2—56	No. 51	2—12	1-59/64
#2—64	No. 50	2-1/4-4-1/2	2-1/32
#3—48	5/64	2-1/2—4	2-1/4
#3—56	No. 46	2-3/4—4	2-1/2
#4—40	No. 43	3—4	2-3/4
#4—48	No. 42		
#5—40	No. 39	**TAPER PIPE**	
#5—44	No. 37		
#6—32	No. 36	1/8—27	R
#6—40	No. 33	1/4—18	7/16
#8—32	No. 29	3/8—18	37/64
#8—36	No. 29	1/2—14	23/32
#10—24	No. 25	3/4—14	59/64
#10—32	No. 21	1—11-1/2	1-5/32
#12—24	No. 17	1¼—11½	1-1/2
#12—28	No. 15	1½—11½	1-47/64
1/4—20	No. 7	2—11-1/2	2-7/32
1/4—28	No. 3	2-1/2—8	2-5/8
5/16—18	F	3—8	3-1/4
5/16—24	I	3-1/2—8	3-3/4
3/8—16	5/16	4—8	4-1/4
3/8—24	Q	5—8	5-9/32
7/16—14	U	6—8	6-11/32
7/16—20	W		
1/2—12	27/64	**STRAIGHT PIPE**	
1/2—13	27/64		
1/2—20	29/64	1/8—27	S
9/16—12	31/64	1/4—18	29/64
9/16—18	33/64	3/8—18	19/32
5/8—11	17/32	1/2—14	47/64
5/8—18	37/64	3/4—14	15/16
3/4—10	21/32	1—11-1/2	1-3/16
3/4—16	11/16	1¼—11½	1-33/64
7/8—9	49/64	1½—11½	1-3/4
7/8—14	13/16	2—11-1/2	2-7/32
1—8	7/8	2-1/2—8	2-21/32
1—12	59/64	3—8	3-9/32
1—14	15/16	3-1/2—8	3-25/32
1-1/8—7	63/64	4—8	4-9/32
1-1/8—12	1-3/64	5—8	5-11/32
1-1/4—7	1-7/64	6—8	6-13/32
1-1/4—12	1-11/64		
1-1/2—6	1-11/32		
1-1/2—12	1-27/64		

Formulas

To compute the speed of a car - Engine speed(rpm) X wheel diameter X .002975 / Rear axle gear ratio

To compute the displacement of an engine - 3.1417 X cylinder radius^2 X Stroke X Number of cylinders

To convert cubic inches to cubic centimeters - multiply by 16.39 or multiply by .01639 to convert to liters

To convert Kilometers to miles - multiply by 5 and divide by 8 (approx.)

To find the circumference of a circle - multiply the diameter by 3.1417

To find the diameter of a circle - mutiply the circumference by .31831

Fasteners

The following types of fasteners may be found in the Classic car. Around 1930, the length of a bolt was measured from top to bottom rather than from the base of the head as today, so lengths shown in your factory literature may not match the new bolts you may buy. Also, hex bolt heads were thicker in the 1920's & early 1930's.

STANDARD HEAD BOLTS AND SCREWS

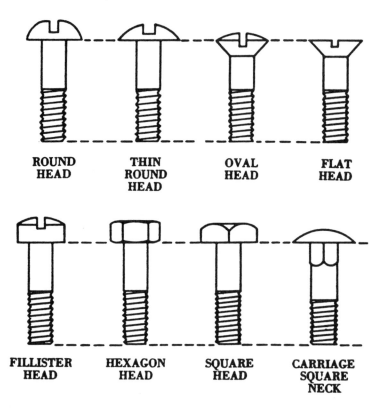

| ROUND HEAD | THIN ROUND HEAD | OVAL HEAD | FLAT HEAD |

| FILLISTER HEAD | HEXAGON HEAD | SQUARE HEAD | CARRIAGE SQUARE NECK |

SAE Grade Code Markings

SAE 0-1-2   SAE 5   SAE 6   SAE 7   SAE 8

DESCRIPTION	GRADE	MATERIAL	STRENGTH
No lines, unmarked Unknown quality	0, 1, 2	Low carbon steel	65,000 psi
Three lines, automotive grade	5	Medium carbon steel	120,000 psi
Four lines, automotive grade	6	Heat treated carbon steel	140,000 psi
Five lines, rarely used	7	Medium carbon alloy steel	140,000 psi
Six lines, best commerical grade	8	Heat treated alloy steel	150,000 psi

Torque Limits in Foot/Pounds

Use these limits as a guide only when the factory or rebuilding shop limits are not indicated

Size	Unknown or SAE Grade 0, 1 & 2 Low Carbon Steel, Tensile Strength 65-75,000 psi	SAE Grade 5 Automotive Grade Medium Carbon Steel, Tensile Strength 120-125,000 psi
1/4-20	5.5	9.7
1/4-28	6.3	11
5/16-18	10	18
5/16-24	13	20
3/8-16	22	39
3/8-24	25	44
7/16-14	32	58
7/16-20	37	69
1/2-13	43	87
1/2-20	50	103
9/16-12	57	110
9/16-18	65	130

BIBLIOGRAPHY

Books

DeAngelis, George. *The Ford Model A As Henry Built It*. Third Edition. South Lyon, Michigan: Motor Cities Publishing, 1983.

Dyke, Andrew L. *Dyke's Automobile Encyclopedia*. Chicago, Illinois: 1932.

Ford Motor Co. *Model A Ford Service Bulletins*. Arcadia, California: Post Era Books, 1972.

Schild, Jim. *Restorer's Model A Shop Manual*. Osceola, Wisconsin: Motorbooks International, 1985.

Schild, Jim. *Restorer's Classic Car Shop Manual*. St. Louis, Missouri: The Auto Review, 1991.

Sorensen, Lorin. *The Commercial Fords*. Helena, California: Silverado Publishing, 1984

Wagner, James K. *Ford Trucks Since 1905*. Glen Ellyn, Illinois: Crestline Publishing, 1978

Periodicals and Catalogs

Ford Motor Co. *Improved Features of the New Ford*. Detroit, Michigan, 1930.

____. *Body Parts List "A" and "AA"*. Detroit, Michigan, 1928-32.

____. *Branch Service Letters*. St. Louis, Missouri, 1928-31.

____. *Model A Sales Catalog*. Detroit, Michigan, 1930-31.

____. *AA Truck Sales Catalog*. Detroit, Michigan, 1931.

____. *Parts Price List, Ford "A" and "AA" 1928-32*. Detroit, Michigan, 1928-32.

____. *The New Ford*, Detroit, Michigan, 1929.

Model A Ford Club of America. *The Model A Judging Standards*. La Habra, California: MARC/MAFCA, 1989.

____. *The Restorer*. La Habra, California, 1970-1993.

Model A Restorer's Club. *The Model A News*. Dearborn, Michigan, 1964-1993.

SERVING BROADER FIELDS

a new light-express body extends the usefulness of Ford Trucks

The Light-express Body equipped with Canopy Top. *A type widely used by hucksters, vendors, grocers and others, for newspaper and magazine deliveries, and for many other purposes. Made of steel, except for floor-boards and sills, which are of specially seasoned wood. The steel end-gate is equipped with heavy chains. Screen sides can be supplied.*

A GROWING number of standard Ford bodies is being made available. Almost daily, they are extending Ford economy to new business fields.

Among these bodies are stake, panel, platform, express and agricultural types, five different dump and four different coal bodies, two police patrols, a funeral coach, an ambulance, a garbage truck, an ice body, and others. With a wide range of choice in style and equipment, they comprise a full line of more than fifty types.

These include trucks, sold complete by all Ford dealers, which have been specifically designed for the requirements of every business. All can be supplied in any color-combination desired.

Ford chassis, too, offer a type for every need. The light-delivery car uses the same chassis as the Model A Ford car. The 1½-ton truck chassis is available with 131½-inch or 157-inch wheelbase. It may be equipped with single or dual rear-wheels, and with high or low rear-axle gear-ratios.

Into the building of both chassis and bodies go fine materials — each selected for

FEATURES
of Ford Commercial Units

Four-cylinder, 40-horse-power engine. Torque-tube drive. Internal-expanding mechanical brakes, all fully enclosed. Forty different kinds of steels for specific purposes. Extensive use of fine steel forgings. More than 20 ball and roller bearings. Three different wheelbases. Two different chassis. Triplex shatter-proof windshields. Low first cost. Low cost of operation and maintenance. Reliability and long life. You may purchase a Ford truck or light commercial car on convenient, economical terms through the Authorized Ford Finance Plans of the Universal Credit Company.

its purpose because it has those qualities of strength, toughness, hardness or flexibility which will serve best in that particular capacity. For example, in the making of the chassis alone, forty different kinds of steel are used.

This is but one example of the value that has been built into it. Others are precision workmanship, and the use of more than twenty ball and roller bearings. These and other features result in completed commercial units that give long, reliable service, capable performance and economy, offering to every business a specialized hauling service at low cost.

Your Ford dealer can supply a chassis and body that are designed for your hauling needs. In New York, Philadelphia, Boston, Detroit, Dallas, and Los Angeles, there are factory exhibits of Ford trucks and light-delivery cars.

For mile after mile of low-cost hauling THE FORD TRUCK

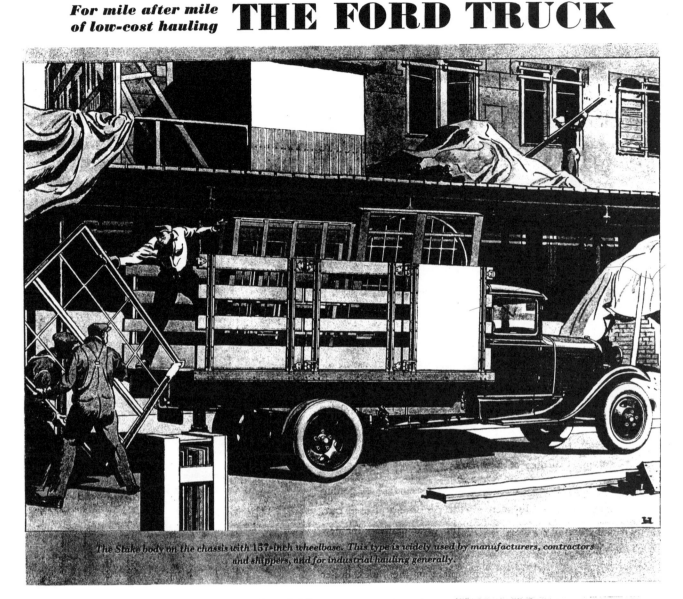

The Stake body on the chassis with 157-inch wheelbase. This type is widely used by manufacturers, contractors and shippers, and for industrial hauling generally.

THE owners of Ford trucks, everywhere, have found that Ford economy goes far beyond the saving in first cost alone. Fine materials, precision-workmanship, and simplicity of construction increase the reliability of Ford units, helping to keep them out of the shop, and on the job. During months of constant use, and thousands of miles of service, their low cost of up-keep becomes a saving of first importance.

Another economical feature of the Ford is the ease with which adjustments or repairs are made. In every locality, there is a nearby Ford dealer who gives prompt and efficient service, at low cost. Because of this, Ford units are seldom idle when there is hauling to be done.

Every day, throughout the country, Ford trucks and delivery cars are serving a larger number of businesses. There is a type specifically adapted for every hauling-purpose.

The Ford 1½-ton truck is available with 131½-inch or 157-inch wheelbase, single or dual rear wheels, high or low rear-axle gear-ratios, open or closed cabs, and with a comprehensive range of bodies.

The light delivery-car, which has the same chassis as the Model A Ford car, can be equipped with bodies to suit any light hauling-requirement.

Your Ford dealer can show you a unit that will do your hauling economically. In New York, Philadelphia, Boston, Detroit, Dallas, and Los Angeles, there are complete Ford commercial exhibits.

FEATURES
of Ford Commercial Units

Four-cylinder, 40-horse-power engine. Torque-tube drive. Internal-expanding mechanical brakes, all fully enclosed. Forty different kinds of steels for specific purposes. Extensive use of fine steel forgings. More than 20 ball and roller bearings. Three different wheelbases. Two different chassis. Triplex shatter-proof windshields. Low first cost. Low cost of operation and maintenance. Reliability and long life. You may purchase a Ford truck or light commercial car on convenient, economical terms through the Authorized Ford Finance Plans of the Universal Credit Company.

Ford

Swiftly and surely, The Ford Truck makes its rounds

FOR the business of quick service, where the trips are short and many, the Ford 1½-ton truck is well suited because of its sturdy design and careful construction. The quick starts, the sudden stops of hauling through heavy traffic serve to emphasize the value of the excellent materials built into the truck.

In such businesses and in numerous others, Ford trucks meet the stern requirements of daily operation through every season with faithful, swift and economical performance.

The engine, for example, develops forty horse-power at 2200 revolutions per minute—a medium engine speed. This, by reducing the wear on moving parts, adds to the life of the truck, while the four-speed transmission increases the range of speed and power. The more than twenty ball and roller bearings, placed at important points throughout chassis and

motor, also ease the strain of schedules that demand speedy and reliable transportation.

Bearings and reciprocating parts are held to close limits of accuracy by means of precision gages in the hands of expert workmen, and extra strength is contributed by the use of forty different kinds of steel in the manufacture of the truck.

Ford trucks are so designed that they can be economically adapted to a large number of businesses. It is possible to procure the Ford truck with a wide variety of bodies, in two different chassis lengths, with single or dual wheels, with open or closed cabs, and with high or low rear axle gear ratios. For light delivery purposes, there is a selection of commercial cars available on the Model A chassis. Go to your Ford dealer, and examine these units in detail.

Ford

FOR EVERY BUSINESS
a specialized hauling-service, at low cost

Heavy-duty express body on the chassis with 131½-inch wheelbase. Made of steel over wood, with an exceedingly strong floor-board construction. Loading space: Length, 102 inches; width, 60 inches; height, 18 inches.

THROUGHOUT the country, Ford trucks have established an important place for themselves in every business field. Their power, speed, reliability, long life, safety, and economy are enabling operators everywhere to move goods from one place to another with a minimum of trouble and expense.

Adding to the value of Ford units is the large number of standard bodies that have been made available. More than forty different types are included, in order to serve every hauling-need.

Both bodies and chassis are built to strictest standards of excellence—in design, materials, and workmanship. Through production in large quantity, economies are effected in the manufac-

ture of these units, which make possible an exceedingly low cost for the completed Ford truck.

FEATURES
of Ford Commercial Units

Four-cylinder, 40-horse-power engine. Torque-tube drive. Internal-expanding mechanical brakes, all fully enclosed. Forty different kinds of steel for specific purposes. Extensive use of fine steel forgings. More than 20 ball and roller bearings. Three different wheelbases. Two different chassis. Triplex shatter-proof windshields. Low first cost. Low cost of operation and maintenance. Reliability and long life. You may purchase a Ford truck or light commercial car on convenient, economical terms through the Authorized Ford Finance Plans of the Universal Credit Company.

Further increasing the adaptability of Ford units is the variety of chassis-equipment available. There is a choice of 131½-inch or 157-inch wheelbase, single or dual rear wheels, and high or low rear-axle gear-ratios.

In addition, there is the light-delivery chassis, which is similar to that of the Model A Ford car, and for which there is a wide variety of body types.

Any Ford dealer can supply a Ford unit, complete, for the specific needs of your business. In Atlanta, Boston, Columbus, Dallas, Detroit, Indianapolis, Los Angeles, New York, New Orleans, Philadelphia, Salt Lake City, Cincinnati, and Cleveland, there are factory exhibits of Ford trucks and light delivery-cars.